D1565339

Robert Louis Stevenson

Selected by
Jenni Calder

PHOENIX
POETRY

This edition first published by Everyman Paperbacks in 1997
Phoenix edition first published in 2003

Selection © J. M. Dent 1997
Chronology © J. M. Dent 2003

ISBN 0 75381 742 X

Typeset by Deltatype Limited, Birkenhead, Merseyside

Printed in China by South China Printing Co. Ltd.
A CIP catalogue reference for this book
is available from the British Library.

The Orion Publishing Group
Orion House
5 Upper St Martin's Lane
London
WC2H 9EA

Contents

from *A Child's Garden of Verses* (1885)

from *Ballads* (1890)

from *Songs of Travel* (1895)

Poems first published in fiction and later poems published posthumously

Robert Louis Stevenson

Early poems published posthumously

Duddingston

1

With caws and chirrupings, the woods
   In this thin sun rejoice,
The Psalm seems but the little kirk
   That sings with its own voice.

The cloud-rifts share their amber light
   With the surface of the mere –
I think the very stones are glad
   To feel each other near.

Once more my whole heart leaps and swells
   And gushes o'er with glee:
The fingers of the sun and shade
   Touch music stops in me.

2

Now fancy paints that bygone day
   When you were here, my fair –
The whole lake rang with rapid skates
   In the windless, winter air.

You leaned to me, I leaned to you,
   Our course was smooth as flight –
We steered – a heel-touch to the left,
   A heel-touch to the right.

We swung our way through flying men,
  Your hand lay fast in mine,
We saw the shifting crowd dispart,
  The level ice-reach shine.

I swear by yon swan-travelled lake,
  By yon calm hill above,
I swear had we been drowned that day
  We had been drowned in love.

The Light-Keeper

I

The brilliant kernel of the night,
The flaming lightroom circles me:
I sit within a blaze of light
Held high above the dusky sea.
Far off the surf doth break and roar
Along bleak miles of moonlit shore,
Where through the tides the tumbling wave
Falls in an avalanche of foam
And drives its churned waters home
Up many an undercliff and cave.

The clear bell chimes: the clockworks strain,
The turning lenses flash and pass,
Frame turning within glittering frame
With frosty gleam of moving glass:
Unseen by me, each dusky hour
The sea-waves welter up the tower
Or in the ebb subside again;
And ever and anon all night,
Drawn from afar by charm of light,
A sea bird beats against the pane.

And lastly when dawn ends the night
And belts the semi-orb of sea,
The tall, pale pharos in the light
Looks white and spectral as may be.
The early ebb is out: the green
Straight belt of seaweed now is seen,
That round the basement of the tower

Marks out the interspace of tide;
And watching men are heavy-eyed,
And sleepless lips are dry and sour.

The night is over like a dream:
The sea-birds cry and dip themselves:
And in the early sunlight, steam
The newly bared and dripping shelves,
Around whose verge the glassy wave
With lisping wash is heard to lave;
While, on the white tower lifted high,
The circling lenses flash and pass
With yellow light in faded glass
And sickly shine against the sky.

2

As the steady lenses circle
With a frosty gleam of glass;
And the clear bell chimes,
And the oil brims over the lip of the burner,
Quiet and still at his desk,
The lonely Light-Keeper
Holds his vigil.

Lured from far,
The bewildered seagull beats
Dully against the lantern;
Yet he stirs not, lifts not his head
From the desk where he reads,
Lifts not his eyes to see
The chill blind circle of night
Watching him through the panes.
This is his country's guardian,

The outmost sentry of peace.
This is the man
Who gives up that is lovely in living
For the means to live.

Poetry cunningly gilds
The life of the Light-Keeper,
Held on high in the blackness
In the burning kernel of night,
The seaman sees and blesses him,
The Poet, deep in a sonnet,
Numbers his inky fingers
Fitly to praise him.
Only we behold him,
Sitting, patient and stolid,
Martyr to a salary.

My brain swims empty and light . . .

My brain swims empty and light
Like a nut on a sea of oil;
And an atmosphere of quiet
Wraps me about from the turmoil and clamour of life.

I stand apart from living,
Apart and holy I stand,
In my new-gained growth of idleness, I stand,
As stood the Shekinah of yore in the holy of holies.

I walk the streets smoking my pipe
And I love the dallying shop-girl
That leans with rounded stern to look at the fashions;
And I hate the bustling citizen,
The eager and hurrying man of affairs I hate,
Because he bears his intolerance writ on his face
And every movement and word of him tells me how
    much he hates me.

I love night in the city,
The lighted streets and the swinging gait of harlots.
I love cool pale morning,
In the empty bye-streets,
With only here and there a female figure,
A slavey with lifted dress and the key in her hand,
A girl or two at play in a corner of waste-land
Tumbling and showing their legs and crying out to me
    loosely.

The Cruel Mistress

Here let me rest, here nurse the uneasy qualm
That yearns within me;
And to the heaped-up sea,
Sun-spangled in the quiet afternoon,
Sing my devotions.

In the sun, at the edge of the down,
The whin-pods crackle
In desultory volleys;
And the bank breathes in my face
Its hot sweet breath –
Breath that stirs and kindles,
Lights that suggest, not satisfy –
Is there never in life or nature
An opiate for desire?
Has everything here a voice,
Saying 'I am not the goal;
Nature is not to be looked at alone;
Her breath, like the breath of a mistress,
Her breath also,
Parches the spirit with longing
Sick and enervating longing.'

Well, let the matter rest.
I rise and brush the windle-straws
Off my clothes; and lighting another pipe
Stretch myself over the down.
Get thee behind me, Nature!
I turn my back on the sun
And face from the grey new town at the foot of the
    bay.

I know an amber lady
Who has her abode
   At the lips of the street
In prisons of coloured glass.
I had rather die of her love
Than sicken for you, O Nature!
Better be drunk and merry
Than dreaming awake!
Better be Falstaff than Obermann!

Storm

The narrow lanes are vacant and wet;
The rough wind bullies and blusters about the
    township.
And spins the vane on the tower
And chases the scurrying leaves,
And the straw in the damp innyard.
See — a girl passes
Tripping gingerly over the pools,
And under her lifted dress
I catch the gleam of a comely, stockinged leg.
Pah! the room stifles me,
Reeking of stale tobacco —
With the four black mealy horrible prints
After Landseer's pictures.
I will go out.

Here the free wind comes with a fuller circle,
Sings, like an angry wasp, in the straining grass,
Sings and whistles;
And the hurried flow of rain
Scourges my face and passes.
Behind me, clustered together, the rain-wet roofs of
    the town
Shine, and the light vane shines as it veers
In the long pale finger of sun that hurries across them
    to me.
The fresh salt air is keen in my nostrils,
And far down the shining sand
Foam and thunder
And take the shape of the bay in eager mirth
The white-head hungry billows.

The earth shakes
As the semicircle of waters
Stoops and casts itself down;
And far outside in the open,
Wandering gleams of sunshine
Show us the ordered horde that hurries to follow.

Ei! merry companions,
Your madness infects me.
My whole soul rises and falls and leaps and tumbles
     with you!
I shout aloud and incite you, O white-headed merry
     companions.
The sight of you alone is better than drinking.
The brazen band is loosened from off my forehead;
My breast and my brain are moistened and cool;
And still I yell in answer
To your hoarse inarticulate voices,
O big, strong, bullying, boisterous waves,
That are of all things in nature the nearest thoughts to
     human,
Because you are wicked and foolish,
Mad and destructive.

Stormy Nights

I cry out war to those who spend their utmost,
Trying to substitute a vain regret
For childhood's vanished moods,
Instead of a full manly satisfaction
In new development.
Their words are vain as the lost shouts,
The wasted breath of solitary hunters
That are far buried in primeval woods –
Clamour that dies in silence,
Cries that bring back no answer
But the great voice of the wind-shaken forest,
Mocking despair.

No – they will get no answer;
For I too recollect,
I recollect and love my perished childhood,
Perfectly love and keenly recollect;
I too remember; and if it could be
Would not recall it.

Do I not know, how, nightly, on my bed
The palpable close darkness shutting round me,
How my small heart went forth to evil things,
How all the possibilities of sin
That were yet present to my innocence
Bound me too narrowly,
And how my spirit beat
The cage of its compulsive purity;
How – my eyes fixed,
My shot lip tremulous between my fingers
I fashioned for myself new modes of crime,

Created for myself with pain and labour
The evil that the cobwebs of society,
The comely secrecies of education,
Had made an itching mystery to meward.

Do I not know again,
When the great winds broke loose and went abroad
At night in the lighted town –
Ah! then it was different –
Then, when I seemed to hear
The storm go by me like a cloak-wrapt horseman
Stooping over the saddle –
Go by, and come again and yet again,
Like some one riding with a pardon,
And ever baffled, ever shut from passage:
Then when the house shook and a horde of noises
Came out and clattered over me all night,
Then, would my heart stand still,
My hair creep fearfully upon my head
And, with my tear-wet face
Buried among the bed-clothes,
Long and bitterly would I pray and wrestle
Till gentle sleep
Threw her great mantle over me,
And my hard breathing gradually ceased.

I was then the Indian,
Well and happy and full of glee and pleasure,
Both hands full of life.
And not without divine impulses
Shot into me by the untried non-ego;
But, like the Indian, too,
Not yet exempt from feverish questionings,
And on my bed of leaves,

Writhing terribly in grasp of terror,
As when the still stars and the great white moon
Watch me athwart black foliage,
Trembling before the interminable vista,
The widening wells of space
In which my thought flags like a wearied bird
In the mid ocean of his autumn flight –
Prostrate before the indefinite great spirit
That the external warder
Plunged like a dagger
Into my bosom.
Now, I am a Greek
White-robed among the sunshine and the statues
And the fair porticos of carven marble –
Fond of olives and dry sherry,
Good tobacco and clever talk with my fellows,
Free from inordinate cravings.
Why would you hurry me, O evangelist,
You with the bands and the shilling packet of tracts
Greatly reduced when taken for distribution?
Why do you taunt my progress,
O green-spectacled Wordsworth! in beautiful verses,
You, the elderly poet?
So I shall travel forward
Step by step with the rest of my race,
In time, if death should spare me,
I shall come on to a farther stage,
And show you St Francis of Assisi.

Song at Dawn

I see the dawn creep round the world,
Here damm'd a moment backward by great hills,
There racing o'er the sea.
Down at the round equator,
It leaps forth straight and rapid,
Driving with firm sharp edge the night before it.
Here gradually it floods
The wooded valleys and the weeds
And the still smokeless cities.
The cocks crow up at the farms;
The sick man's spirit is glad;
The watch treads brisker about the dew-wet deck;
The light-keeper locks his desk,
As the lenses turn,
Faded and yellow.

The girl with the embroidered shift
Rises and leans on the sill,
And her full bosom heaves
Drinking deep of the silentness.
I too rise and watch
The healing fingers of dawn –
I too drink from its eyes
The unaccountable peace –
I too drink and am satisfied as with food.
Fain would I go
Down by the winding crossroad by the trees,
Where at the corner of wet wood
The blackbird in the early grey and stillness
Wakes his first song.

Peace, who can make verses clink,
Find ictus following surely after ictus,
At such an hour as this, the heart
Lies steeped and silent.
O dreaming, leaning girl,
Already the grey passes, the white streak
Brightens above dark woodlands, Day begins.

To the Commissioners of Northern Lights, with a Paper

I send to you, commissioners,
A paper that may please ye, sirs,
(For troth they say it micht be worse
    An' I believ't)
And on your business lay my curse
    Before I leav't.

I thocht I'd serve wi' you, sirs, yince,
But I've thocht better of it since;
The maitter I will nowise mince,
    But tell ye true:
I'll service wi' some ither prince,
    An' no' wi' you.

I've no' been very deep, ye'll think,
Cam' delicately to the brink
An' when the water gart me shrink
    Straucht took the rue,
An' didna stoop my fill to drink –
    I own it true.

I kent on cape and isle, a light
Burnt fair an' clearly ilka night;
But at the service I took fright,
    As sune's I saw,
An' being still a neophite
    Gaed straucht awa'.

Anither course I now begin,
  The weeg I'll cairry for my sin,
  The court my voice sall echo in,
     An' − wha can tell? −
Some ither day I may be yin
     O' you mysel'.

To Charles Baxter

Noo lyart leaves blaw ower the green,
Reid are the bonny woods o' Dean,
An' here we're back in Embro, frien',
      To pass the winter.
Whilk noo, wi' frosts afore, draws in,
      An' snaws ahint her.

I've seen 's hae days to fricht us a',
The Pentlands poothered weel wi' snaw,
The ways half smoored wi' liquid thaw
      An' half congealin',
The snell an' scowtherin' norther blaw
      Frae blae Brunteelan'.

I've seen 's been unco sweir to sally
And at the door-cheeks daff an' dally –
Seen 's daidle thus an' shilly-shally
      For near a minute –
Sae cauld the wind blew up the valley,
      The deil was in it! –

Syne spread the silk an' tak the gate,
In blast an' blaudin' rain, deil hae 't!
The hale toon glintin', stane an' slate,
      Wi' cauld an' weet,
An' to the Court, gin we 'se be late,
      Bicker oor feet.

And at the Court, tae, aft I saw
Whaur Advocates by twa an' twa
Gang gesterin' end to end the ha'

In weeg an' goon,
To crack o' what ye wull but Law
    The hale forenoon.

That muckle ha', maist like a kirk,
I've kent at braid mid-day sae mirk
Ye'd seen white weegs an' faces lurk
    Like ghaists frae Hell,
But whether Christian ghaists or Turk
    Deil ane could tell.

The three fires lunted in the gloom,
The wind blew like the blast o' doom,
The rain upo' the roof abune
    Played Peter Dick –
Ye wad nae'd licht enough i' the room
    Your teeth to pick!

But, freend, ye ken how me an' you,
The ling-lang lanely winter through,
Keep'd a guid speerit up, an' true
    To lore Horatian,
We aye the ither bottle drew –
    To inclination.

Sae let us in the comin' days
Stand sicker on oor auncient ways –
The strauchtest road in a' the maze
    Since Eve ate apples;
An' let the winter weet oor cla'es –
    We'll weet oor thrapples.

from Underwoods (1887)

A Song of the Road

The gauger walked with willing foot,
And aye the gauger played the flute;
And what should Master Gauger play
But *Over the hills and far away*?

When'er I buckle on my pack
And foot it gaily in the track,
O pleasant gauger, long since dead,
I hear you fluting on ahead.

You go with me the self-same way –
The self-same air for me you play;
For I do think and so do you
It is the tune to travel to.

For who would gravely set his face
To go to this or t'other place?
There's nothing under Heav'n so blue
That's fairly worth the travelling to.

On every hand the roads begin,
And people walk with zeal therein;
But wheresoe'er the highways tend,
Be sure there's nothing at the end.

Then follow you, wherever hie
The travelling mountains of the sky.
Or let the streams in civil mode
Direct your choice upon a road;

For one and all, or high or low,
Will lead you where you wish to go;
  And one and all go night and day
  Over the hills and far away!

The House Beautiful

A naked house, a naked moor,
A shivering pool before the door,
A garden bare of flowers and fruit
And poplars at the garden foot:
Such is the place that I live in,
Bleak without and bare within.

Yet shall your ragged moor receive
The incomparable pomp of eve,
And the cold glories of the dawn
Behind your shivering trees be drawn;
And when the wind from place to place
Doth the unmoored cloud-galleons chase,
Your garden gloom and gleam again,
With leaping sun, with glancing rain.
Here shall the wizard moon ascend
The heavens, in the crimson end
Of day's declining splendour; here
The army of the stars appear.
The neighbour hollows dry or wet,
Spring shall with tender flowers beset;
And oft the morning muser see
Larks rising from the broomy lea,
And every fairy wheel and thread
Of cobweb dew-bediamonded.
When daisies go, shall winter time
Silver the simple grass with rime;
Autumnal frosts enchant the pool
And make the cart-ruts beautiful;
And when snow-bright the moor expands,
How shall your children clap their hands!

To make this earth, our hermitage,
A cheerful and a changeful page,
God's bright and intricate device
Of days and seasons doth suffice.

To Will H. Low

Youth now flees on feathered foot,
Faint and fainter sounds the flute,
Rarer songs of gods; and still
Somewhere on the sunny hill,
Or along the winding stream,
Through the willows, flits a dream;
Flits but shows a smiling face,
Flees but with so quaint a grace,
None can choose to stay at home,
All must follow, all must roam.

This is unborn beauty: she
Now in air floats high and free,
Takes the sun and breaks the blue; –
Late with stooping pinion flew
Raking hedgerow trees, and wet
Her wing in silver streams, and set
Shining foot on temple roof:
Now again she flies aloof,
Coasting mountain clouds and kiss't
By the evening's amethyst.

In wet wood and miry lane,
Still we pant and pound in vain;
Still with leaden foot we chase
Waning pinion, fainting face;
Still with gray hair we stumble on,
Till, behold, the vision gone!
Where hath fleeting beauty led?
To the doorway of the dead.
Life is over, life was gay:
We have come the primrose way.

To Mrs Will H. Low

Even in the bluest noonday of July,
There could not run the smallest breath of wind
But all the quarter sounded like a wood;
And in the chequered silence and above
The hum of city cabs that sought the Bois,
Suburban ashes shivered into song.
A patter and a chatter and a chirp
And a long dying hiss – it was as though
Starched old brocaded dames through all the house
Had trailed a strident skirt, or the whole sky
Even in a wink had over-brimmed in rain.
Hark, in these shady parlours, how it talks
Of the near Autumn, how the smitten ash
Trembles and augurs floods! O not too long
In these inconstant latitudes delay,
O not too late from the unbeloved north
Trim your escape! For soon shall this low roof
Resound indeed with rain, soon shall your eyes
Search the foul garden, search the darkened rooms,
Nor find one jewel but the blazing log.

To Andrew Lang

Dear Andrew, with the brindled hair,
Who glory to have thrown in air,
High over arm, the trembling reed,
By Ale and Kail, by Till and Tweed:
An equal craft of hand you show
The pen to guide, the fly to throw:
I count you happy starred; for God,
When He with inkpot and with rod
Endowed you, bade your fortune lead
Forever by the crooks of Tweed,
Forever by the woods of song
And lands that to the Muse belong;
Or if in peopled streets, or in
The abhorred pedantic sanhedrin,
It should be yours to wander, still
Airs of the morn, airs of the hill,
The plovery Forest and the seas
That break about the Hebrides,
Should follow over field and plain
And find you at the window pane;
And you again see hill and peel,
And the bright springs gush at your heel.
So went the fiat forth, and so
Garrulous like a brook you go,
With sound of happy mirth and sheen
Of daylight – whether by the green
You fare that moment, or the gray;
Whether you dwell in March or May;
Or whether treat of reels and rods
Or of the old unhappy gods:
Still like a brook your page has shone,
And your ink sings of Helicon.

To W. E. Henley

The year runs through her phases; rain and sun,
Springtime and summer pass; winter succeeds;
But one pale season rules the house of death.
Cold falls the imprisoned daylight; fell disease
By each lean pallet squats, and pain and sleep
Toss gaping on the pillows.

                         But O thou!
Uprise and take thy pipe. Bid music flow,
Strains by good thoughts attended, like the spring
The swallows follow over land and sea.
Pain sleeps at once; at once, with open eyes,
Dozing despair awakes. The shepherd sees
His flock come bleating home; the seaman hears
Once more the cordage rattle. Airs of home!
Youth, love and roses blossom; the gaunt ward
Dislimns and disappears, and, opening out,
Shows brooks and forests, and the blue beyond
Of mountains.

                 Small the pipe; but O! do thou,
Peak-faced and suffering piper, blow therein
The dirge of heroes dead; and to these sick,
These dying, sound the triumph over death.
Behold! each greatly breathes; each tastes a joy
Unknown before, in dying; for each knows
A hero dies with him – though unfulfilled,
Yet conquering truly – and not dies in vain.

So is pain cheered, death comforted; the house
Of sorrow smiles to listen. Once again –
O thou, Orpheus and Heracles, the bard
And the deliverer, touch the stops again!

Henry James

Who comes tonight? We ope the doors in vain.
Who comes? My bursting walls, can you contain
The presences that now together throng
Your narrow entry, as with flowers and song,
As with the air of life, the breath of talk?
Lo, how these fair immaculate women walk
Behind their jocund maker; and we see
Slighted *De Mauves*, and that far different she,
Gressie, the trivial sphynx; and to our feast
Daisy and *Barb* and *Chancellor* (she not least!)
With all their silken, all their airy kin,
Do like unbidden angels enter in.
But he, attended by these shining names,
Comes (best of all) himself – our welcome James.

The Mirror Speaks

Where the bells peal far at sea
Cunning fingers fashioned me.
There on palace walls I hung
While that Consuelo sung;
But I heard, though I listened well,
Never a note, never a trill,
Never a beat of the chiming bell.
There I hung and looked, and there
In my gray face, faces fair
Shone from under shining hair.
Well I saw the poising head,
But the lips moved and nothing said;
And when lights were in the hall,
Silent moved the dancers all.

So awhile I glowed, and then
Fell on dusty days and men;
Long I slumbered packed in straw,
Long I none but dealers saw;
Till before my silent eye
One that sees came passing by.

Now with an outlandish grace,
To the sparkling fire I face
In the blue room at Skerryvore;
Where I wait until the door
Open, and the Prince of Men,
Henry James, shall come again.

Requiem

Under the wide and starry sky,
Dig the grave and let me lie.
Glad did I live and gladly die,
    And I laid me down with a will.

This be the verse you grave for me:
Here he lies where he longed to be;
Home is the sailor, home from sea,
    And the hunter home from the hill.

The Celestial Surgeon

If I have faltered more or less
In my great task of happiness;
If I have moved among my race
And shown no glorious morning face;
If beams from happy human eyes
Have moved me not; if morning skies,
Books, and my food, and summer rain
Knocked on my sullen heart in vain:
Lord, thy most pointed pleasure take
And stab my spirit broad awake;
Or, Lord, if too obdurate I,
Choose thou, before that spirit die,
A piercing pain, a killing sin,
And to my dead heart run them in!

In Memoriam F. A. S.

Yet, O stricken heart, remember, O remember
  How of human days he lived the better part.
April came to bloom and never dim December
  Breathed its killing chills upon the head or heart.

Doomed to know not Winter, only Spring, a being
  Trod the flowery April blithely for a while,
Took his fill of music, joy of thought and seeing,
  Came and stayed and went, nor ever ceased to smile.

Came and stayed and went, and now when all is
    finished,
  You alone have crossed the melancholy stream,
Yours the pang, but his, O his, the undiminished
  Undecaying gladness, undeparted dream.

All that life contains of torture, toil, and treason,
  Shame, dishonour, death, to him were but a name.
Here, a boy, he dwelt through all the singing season
  And ere the day of sorrow departed as he came.

To My Father

Peace and her huge invasion to these shores
Puts daily home; innumerable sails
Dawn on the far horizon and draw near;
Innumerable loves, uncounted hopes
To our wild coasts, not darkling now, approach:
Not now obscure, since thou and thine are there,
And bright on the lone isle, the foundered reef,
The long, resounding foreland, Pharos stands.

These are thy works, O father, these thy crown;
Whether on high the air be pure, they shine
Along the yellowing sunset, and all night
Among the unnumbered stars of God they shine;
Or whether fogs arise and far and wide
The low sea-level drown – each finds a tongue
And all night long the tolling bell resounds:
So shine, so toll, till night be overpast,
Till the star vanish, till the sun return,
And in the haven rides the fleet secure.

In the first hour, the seaman in his skiff
Moves through the unmoving bay, to where the town
Its earliest smoke into the air upbreathes
And the rough hazels climb along the beach.
To the tugg'd oar the distant echo speaks.
The ship lies resting, where by reef and roost
Thou and thy lights have led her like a child.

This hast thou done, and I – can I be base?
I must arise, O father, and to port
Some lost, complaining seaman pilot home.

A Portrait

I am a kind of farthing dip,
   Unfriendly to the nose and eyes;
A blue-behinded ape, I skip
   Upon the trees of Paradise.

At mankind's feast, I take my place
   In solemn, sanctimonious state,
And have the air of saying grace
   While I defile the dinner plate.

I am 'the smiler with the knife',
   The battener upon garbage, I –
Dear Heaven, with such a rancid life,
   Were it not better far to die?

Yet still, about the human pale,
   I love to scamper, love to race,
To swing by my irreverent tail
   All over the most holy place;

And when at length, some golden day,
   The unfailing sportsman, aiming at,
Shall bag, me – all the world shall say:
   Thank God, and there's an end of that!

A Camp

The bed was made, the room was fit,
By punctual eve the stars were lit;
The air was still, the water ran,
No need was there for maid or man,
When we put up, my ass and I,
At God's green caravanserai.

The Country of the Camisards

We travelled in the print of olden wars,
  Yet all the land was green,
  And love we found, and peace,
  Where fire and war had been.

They pass and smile, the children of the sword –
  No more the sword they wield;
  And O, how deep the corn
  Along the battlefield!

Skerryvore

For love of lovely words, and for the sake
Of those, my kinsmen and my countrymen,
Who early and late in the windy ocean toiled
To plant a star for seamen, where was then
The surfy haunt of seals and cormorants:
I, on the lintel of this cot, inscribe
The name of a strong tower.

Skerryvore: The Parallel

Here all is sunny, and when the truant gull
Skims the green level of the lawn, his wing
Dispetals roses; here the house is framed
Of kneaded brick and the plumed mountain pine,
Such clay as artists fashion and such wood
As the tree-climbing urchin breaks. But there
Eternal granite hewn from the living isle
And dowelled with brute iron, rears a tower
That from its wet foundation to its crown
Of glittering glass, stands, in the sweep of winds,
Immovable, immortal, eminent.

My House, I say . . .

My house, I say. But hark to the sunny doves
That make my roof the arena of their loves,
That gyre about the gable all day long
And fill the chimneys with their murmurous song:
Our house, they say; and mine, the cat declares
And spreads his golden fleece upon the chairs;
And mine the dog, and rises stiff with wrath
If any alien foot profane the path.
So too the buck that trimmed my terraces,
Our whilome gardener, called the garden his;
Who now, deposed, surveys my plain abode
And his late kingdom, only from the road.

Say not of me . . .

Say not of me that weakly I declined
The labours of my sires, and fled the sea,
The towers we founded and the lamps we lit,
To play at home with paper like a child.
But rather say: In the afternoon of time
A strenuous family dusted from its hands
The sand of granite, and beholding far
Along the sounding coast its pyramids
And tall memorials catch the dying sun,
Smiled well content, and to this childish task
Around the fire addressed its evening hours.

The Maker to Posterity

Far 'yont amang the years to be
When a' we think, an' a' we see,
An' a' we luve, 's been dung ajee
    By time's rouch shouther,
An' what was richt and wrang for me
    Lies mangled throu'ther,

It's possible — it's hardly mair —
That some ane, ripin' after lear —
Some auld professor or young heir,
    If still there's either —
May find an' read me, an' be sair
    Perplexed, puir brither!

'What tongue does your auld bookie speak?'
He'll spier; an' I, his mou to steik:
'No bein' fit to write in Greek,
    I wrote in Lallan,
Dear to my heart as the peat reek,
    Auld as Tantallon.

'Few spak it than, an' noo there's nane.
My puir auld sangs lie a' their lane,
Their sense, that aince was braw an' plain,
    Tint a'thegether,
Like runes upon a standin' stane
    Amang the heather.

'But think not you the brae to speel;
You, tae, maun chow the bitter peel;
For a' your lear, for a' your skeel,

Ye're nane sae lucky;
An' things are mebbe waur than weel
　　For you, my buckie.

'The hale concern (baith hens an' eggs,
Baith books an' writers, stars an' clegs)
Noo stachers upon lowsent legs
　　An' wears awa';
The tack o' mankind, near the dregs,
　　Rins unco' law.

'Your book, that in some braw new tongue,
Ye wrote or prentit, preached or sung,
Will still be just a bairn, an' young
　　In fame an' years,
Whan the hale planet's guts are dung
　　About your ears;

'An' you, sair gruppin' to a spar
Or whammled wi' some bleezin' star,
Cryin' to ken whaur deil ye are,
　　Hame, France, or Flanders —
Whang sindry like a railway car
　　An' flie in danders.'

Ille Terrarum

Frae nirly, nippin', Eas'lan' breeze,
Frae Norlan' snaw, an' haar o' seas,
Weel happit in your gairden trees,
    A bonny bit,
Atween the muckly Pentland's knees,
    Secure ye sit.

Beeches an' aiks entwine their theek,
An' firs, a stench, auld-farrant clique.
A' simmer day, your chimleys reek,
    Couthy and bien;
An' here an' there your windies keek
    Amang the green.

A pickle plats an' paths an' posies,
A wheen auld gillyflowers an' roses:
A ring o' wa's the hale encloses
    Frae sheep or men;
An' there the auld housie beeks an' dozes,
    A' by her lane.

The gairdner crooks his weary back
A' day in the pitaty-track,
Or mebbe stops awhile to crack
    Wi' Jane the cook,
Or at some buss, worm-eaten-black,
    To gie a look.

Frae the high hills the curlew ca's;
The sheep gang baaing by the wa's;
Or whiles a clan o' roosty craws

Cangle thegether;
The wild bees seek the gairden raws,
        Weariet wi' heather.

Or in the gloamin' douce an' gray
The sweet-throat mavis tunes her lay;
The herd comes likin' doun the brae;
        An' by degrees
The muckle siller müne maks way
        Amang the trees.

Here aft hae I, wi' sober heart,
For meditation sat apairt,
When orra loves or kittle art
        Perplexed my mind;
Here socht a balm for ilka smart
        O' humankind.

Here aft, weel neukit by my lane,
Wi' Horace, or perhaps Montaigne,
The mornin' hours hae come an' gane
        Abüne my heid –
I wadnae gi'en a chucky-stane
        For a' I'd read.

But noo the auld city, street by street,
An' winter fu' o' snaw an' sleet,
Awhile shut in my gangrel feet
        An' goavin' mettle;
Noo is the soopit ingle sweet,
        An' liltin' kettle.

An' noo the winter winds complain;
Cauld lies the glaur in ilka lane;
On draigled hizzie, tautit wean
        An' drucken lads,
In the mirk nicht, the winter rain
        Dribbles an' blads.

Whan bugles frae the Castle rock,
An' beaten drums wi' dowie shock,
Wauken, at cauld-rife sax o'clock,
        My chitterin' frame,
I mind me on the kintry cock,
        The kintry hame.

I mind me on yon bonny bield;
An' Fancy traivels far afield
To gaither a' that gairdens yield
        O' sun an' Simmer:
To hearten up a dowie chield,
        Fancy's the limmer!

A Mile an' a Bittock

A mile an' a bittock, a mile or twa,
Abüne the burn, ayont the law,
Davie an' Donal' an' Cherlie an' a',
    An' the müne was shinin' clearly!

Ane went hame wi' the ither, an' then
The ither went hame wi' the ither twa men,
An' baith wad return him the service again,
    An' the müne was shinin' clearly!

The clocks were chappin' in house an' ha',
Eleeven, twal an' ane an' twa;
An' the guidman's face was turnt to the wa',
    An' the müne was shinin' clearly!

A wind got up frae affa the sea,
It blew the stars as clear's could be,
It blew in the een of a' o' the three,
    An' the müne was shinin' clearly!

Noo, Davie was first to get sleep in his head,
'The best o' frien's maun twine,' he said;
'I'm weariet, an' here I'm awa' to my bed.'
    An' the müne was shinin' clearly!

Twa o' them walkin' an' crackin' their lane,
The mornin' licht cam gray an' plain,
An' the birds they yammert on stick an' stane,
    An' the müne was shinin' clearly!

O years ayont, O years awa',
My lads, ye'll mind whate'er befa' –
My lads, ye'll mind on the bield o' the law,
    When the müne was shinin' clearly.

A Lowden Sabbath Morn

The clinkum-clank o' Sabbath bells
Noo to the hoastin' rookery swells,
Noo faintin' laigh in shady dells,
    Sounds far an' near,
An' through the simmer kintry tells
    Its tale o' cheer.

An' noo, to that melodious play,
A' deidly awn the quiet sway –
A' ken their solemn holiday,
    Bestial an' human,
The singin' lintie on the brae,
    The restin' plou'man.

He, mair than a' the lave o' men,
His week completit joys to ken;
Half-dressed, he daunders out an' in,
    Perplext wi' leisure;
An' his raxt limbs he'll rax again
    Wi' painfu' pleesure.

The steerin' mither strange afit
Noo shoos the bairnies but a bit;
Noo cries them ben, their Sinday shüit
    To scart upon them,
Or sweeties in their pouch to pit,
    Wi' blessin's on them.

The lasses, clean frae tap to taes,
Are busked in crunklin' underclaes;
The gartened hose, the weel-filled stays,

                The nakit shift,
A' bleached on bonny greens for days,
                An' white's the drift.

An' noo to face the kirkward mile:
The guidman's hat o' dacent style,
The blackit shoon, we noo maun fyle
                As white's the miller:
A waefu' peety tae, to spile
                The warth o' siller.

Our Marg'et, aye sae keen to crack,
Douce-stappin' in the stoury track,
Her emeralt goun a' kiltit back
                Frae snawy coats,
White-ankled, leads the kirkward pack
                Wi' Dauvit Groats.

A thocht ahint, in runkled breeks,
A' spiled wi' lyin' by for weeks,
The guidman follows closs, an' cleiks
                The sonsie missis;
His sarious face at aince bespeaks
                The day that this is.

And aye an' while we nearer draw
To whaur the kirkton lies alaw,
Mair neebours, comin' saft an' slaw
                Frae here an' there,
The thicker thrang the gate an' caw
                The stour in air.

But hark! the bells frae nearer clang;
To rowst the slaw, their sides they bang;
An' see! black coats a'ready thrang
      The green kirkyaird;
And at the yett, the chestnuts sprang
      That brocht the laird.

The solemn elders at the plate
Stand drinkin' deep the pride o' state:
The practised hands as gash an' great
      As Lords o' Session;
The later named, a wee thing blate
      In their expression.

The prentit stanes that mark the deid,
Wi' lengthened lip, the sarious read;
Syne wag a moraleesin' heid,
      An' then an' there
Their hirplin' practice an' their creed
      Try hard to square.

It's here our Merren lang has lain,
A wee bewast the table-stane;
An' yon's the grave o' Sandy Blane;
      An' further ower,
The mither's brithers, dacent men!
      Lie a' the fower.

Here the guidman sall bide awee
To dwall amang the deid; to see
Auld faces clear in fancy's e'e;
      Belike to hear
Auld voices fa'in saft an' slee
      On fancy's ear.

Thus, on the day o' solemn things,
The bell that in the steeple swings
To fauld a scaittered faim'ly rings
        Its walcome screed;
An' just a wee thing nearer brings
        The quick an' deid.

But noo the bell is ringin' in;
To tak their places, folk begin;
The minister himsel' will shüne
        Be up the gate,
Filled fu' wi' clavers about sin
        An' man's estate.

The tünes are up – French, to be shüre,
The faithfü' French, an' twa-three mair;
The auld prezentor, hoastin' sair,
        Wales out the portions,
An' yirks the tüne into the air
        Wi' queer contortions.

Follow the prayer, the readin' next,
An' than the fisslin' for the text –
The twa-three last to find it, vext
        But kind o' proud;
An' than the peppermints are raxed,
        An' southernwood.

For noo's the time whan pows are seen
Nid noddin' like a mandareen;
When tenty mithers stap a preen
        In sleepin' weans;
An' nearly half the parochine
        Forget their pains.

There's just a waukrif' twa or three:
Thrawn commentautors sweet to 'gree,
Weans glowrin' at the bumlin' bee
          On windie-glasses,
Or lads that tak a keek a-glee
          At sonsie lasses.

Himsel', meanwhile, frae whaur he cocks
An' bobs belaw the soundin'-box,
The treesures of his words unlocks
          Wi' prodigality,
An' deals some unco dingin' knocks
          To infidality.

Wi' sappy unction, hoo he burkes
The hopes o' men that trust in works,
Expounds the fau'ts o' ither kirks,
          An' shaws the best o' them
No muckle better than mere Turks,
          When a's confessed o' them.

Bethankit! what a bonny creed!
What mair would ony Christian need? –
The braw words rumm'le ower his heid,
          Nor steer the sleeper;
And in their restin' graves, the deid
          Sleep aye the deeper.

The Spaewife

O, I wad like to ken – to the beggar-wife says I –
Why chops are guid to brander and nane sae guid to
    fry.
An' siller, that's sae braw to keep, is brawer still to
    gi'e.
– It's *gey an' easy spierin'*, says the beggar-wife to me.

O, I wad like to ken – to the beggar-wife says I –
Hoo a' things come to be whaur we find them when
    we try,
The lasses in their claes an' the fishes in the sea.
– It's *gey an' easy spierin'*, says the beggar-wife to me.

O, I wad like to ken – to the beggar-wife says I –
Why lads are a' to sell an' lasses a' to buy;
An' naebody for dacency but barely twa or three.
– It's *gey an' easy spierin'*, says the beggar-wife to me.

O, I wad like to ken – to the beggar-wife says I –
Gin death's as shüre to men as killin' is to kye,
Why God has filled the yearth sae fu' o' tasty things to
    pree.
– It's *gey an' easy spierin'*, says the beggar-wife to me.

O, I wad like to ken – to the beggar-wife says I –
The reason o' the cause an' the wherefore o' the why,
Wi' mony anither riddle brings the tears into my e'e.
– It's *gey an' easy spierin'*, says the beggar-wife to me.

My Conscience!

Of a' the ills that flesh can fear,
The loss o' frien's, the lack o' gear,
A yowlin' tyke, a glandered mear,
      A lassie's nonsense –
There's just ae thing I cannae bear,
      An' that's my conscience.

Whan day (an' a' excüse) has gane,
An' wark is düne, and duty's plain,
An' to my chalmer a' my lane
      I creep apairt,
My conscience! hoo the yammerin' pain
      Stends to my heart!

An' day wi' various ends in view
The hairsts o' time I had to pu',
An' made a hash wad staw a soo,
      Let be a man! –
My conscience! whan my han's were fu',
      Whaur were ye than?

An' there were a' the lures o' life,
There pleesure skirlin' on the fife,
There anger, wi' the hotchin' knife
      Ground shairp in Hell –
My conscience! – you that's like a wife! –
      Whaur was yoursel'?

I ken it fine: just waitin' here,
To gar the evil waur appear,
To clart the guid, confüse the clear,

Mis-ca' the great,
My conscience! an' to raise a steer
        Whan a's ower late.

Sic-like, some tyke grawn auld and blind,
Whan thieves brok' through the gear to p'ind,
Has lain his dozened length an' grinned
        At the disaster;
An' the morn's mornin', wud's the wind,
        Yokes on his master.

from *A Child's Garden of Verses* (1885)

Pirate Story

Three of us afloat in the meadow by the swing,
   Three of us aboard in the basket on the lea.
Winds are in the air, they are blowing in the spring,
   And waves are on the meadow like the waves there
      are at sea.

Where shall we adventure, today that we're afloat,
   Wary of the weather and steering by a star?
Shall it be to Africa, a-steering of the boat,
   To Providence, or Babylon, or off to Malabar?

Hi! but here's a squadron a-rowing on the sea –
   Cattle on the meadow a-charging with a roar!
Quick, and we'll escape them, they're as mad as they
      can be,
   The wicket is the harbour and the garden is the
      shore.

Windy Nights

Whenever the moon and stars are set,
　　Whenever the wind is high,
All night long in the dark and wet,
　　A man goes riding by.
Late in the night when the fires are out,
Why does he gallop and gallop about?

Whenever the trees are crying aloud,
　　And ships are tossed at sea,
By, on the highway, low and loud,
　　By at the gallop goes he.
By at the gallop he goes, and then
By he comes back at the gallop again.

Travel

I should like to rise and go
Where the golden apples grow;
Where below another sky
Parrot islands anchored lie,
And, watched by cockatoos and goats,
Lonely Crusoes building boats;
Where in sunshine reaching out
Eastern cities, miles about,
Are with mosque and minaret
Among sandy gardens set,
And the rich goods from near and far
Hang for sale in the bazaar;
Where the Great Wall round China goes,
And on one side the desert blows,
And with bell and voice and drum,
Cities on the other hum;
Where are forests, hot as fire,
Wide as England, tall as a spire,
Full of apes and cocoa-nuts
And the negro hunters' huts;
Where the knotty crocodile
Lies and blinks in the Nile,
And the red flamingo flies
Hunting fish before his eyes;
Where in jungles, near and far,
Man-devouring tigers are,
Lying close and giving ear
Lest the hunt be drawing near,
Or a comer-by be seen
Swinging in a palanquin;
Where among the desert sands

Some deserted city stands,
All its children, sweep and prince,
Grown to manhood ages since,
Not a foot in street or house,
Not a stir of child or mouse,
And when kindly falls the night,
In all the town no spark of light.
There I'll come when I'm a man
With a camel caravan;
Light a fire in the gloom
Of some dusty dining-room;
See the pictures on the walls,
Heroes, fights and festivals;
And in a corner find the toys
Of the old Egyptian boys.

Where Go the Boats?

Dark brown is the river,
  Golden is the sand.
It flows along for ever,
  With trees on either hand.

Green leaves a-floating,
  Castles of the foam,
Boats of mine a-boating –
  Where will all come home?

On goes the river
  And out past the mill,
Away down the valley,
  Away down the hill.

Away down the river,
  A hundred miles or more,
Other little children
  Shall bring my boats ashore.

The Land of Counterpane

When I was sick and lay a-bed,
I had two pillows at my head,
And all my toys beside me lay
To keep me happy all the day.

And sometimes for an hour or so
I watched my leaden soldiers go,
With different uniforms and drills,
Among the bed-clothes, through the hills;

And sometimes sent my ships in fleets
All up and down among the sheets;
Or brought my trees and houses out,
And planted cities all about.

I was the giant great and still
That sits upon the pillow-hill,
And sees before him, dale and plain,
The pleasant land of counterpane.

My Shadow

I have a little shadow that goes in and out with me,
And what can be the use of him is more than I can
  see.
He is very, very like me from the heels up to the
  head;
And I see him jump before me, when I jump into my
  bed.

The funniest thing about him is the way he likes to
  grow —
Not at all like proper children, which is always very
  slow;
For he sometimes shoots up taller like an india-rubber
  ball,
And he sometimes gets so little that there's none of
  him at all.

He hasn't got a notion of how children ought to play,
And can only make a fool of me in every sort of way.
He stays so close beside me, he's a coward you can
  see;
I'd think shame to stick to nursie as that shadow sticks
  to me!

One morning, very early, before the sun was up,
I rose and found the shining dew on every buttercup;
But my lazy little shadow, like an arrant sleepy-head,
Had stayed at home behind me and was fast asleep in
  bed.

Happy Thought

The world is so full of a number of things,
I'm sure we should all be as happy as kings.

Keepsake Mill

Over the borders, a sin without pardon,
  Breaking the branches and crawling below,
Out through the breach in the wall of the garden,
  Down by the banks of the river, we go.

Here is the mill with the humming of thunder,
  Here is the weir with the wonder of foam,
Here is the sluice with the race running under –
  Marvellous places, though handy to home!

Sounds of the village grow stiller and stiller,
  Stiller the note of the birds on the hill;
Dusty and dim are the eyes of the miller,
  Deaf are his ears with the moil of the mill.

Years may go by, and the wheel in the river
  Wheel as it wheels for us, children, today,
Wheel and keep roaring and foaming for ever
  Long after all of the boys are away.

Home from the Indies and home from the ocean,
  Heroes and soldiers we all shall come home;
Still we shall find the old mill wheel in motion,
  Turning and churning that river to foam.

You with the bean that I gave when we quarrelled,
  I with your marble of Saturday last,
Honoured and old and all gaily apparelled,
  Here we shall meet and remember the past.

The Lamplighter

My tea is nearly ready and the sun has left the sky;
It's time to take the window to see Leerie going by;
For every night at teatime and before you take your
  seat,
With lantern and with ladder he comes posting up the
  street.

Now Tom would be a driver and Maria go to sea,
And my papa's a banker and as rich as he can be;
But I, when I am stronger and can choose what I'm to
  do,
O Leerie, I'll go round at night and light the lamps
  with you!

For we are very lucky, with a lamp before the door,
And Leerie stops to light it as he lights so many more;
And O! before you hurry by with ladder and with
  light,
O Leerie, see a little child and nod to him tonight!

From a Railway Carriage

Faster than fairies, faster than witches,
Bridges and houses, hedges and ditches;
And charging along like troops in a battle,
All through the meadows the horses and cattle:
All of the sights of the hill and the plain
Fly as thick as driving rain;
And ever again, in the wink of an eye,
Painted stations whistle by.

Here is a child who clambers and scrambles,
All by himself and gathering brambles;
Here is a tramp who stands and gazes;
And there is the green for stringing the daisies!
Here is a cart run away in the road
Lumping along with man and load;
And here is a mill and there is a river:
Each a glimpse and gone for ever!

North-West Passage

1 GOOD NIGHT

When the bright lamp is carried in,
The sunless hours again begin;
O'er all without, in field and lane,
The haunted night returns again.

Now we behold the embers flee
About the firelit hearth; and see
Our faces painted as we pass,
Like pictures, on the window-glass.

Must we to bed indeed? Well then,
Let us arise and go like men,
And face with an undaunted tread
The long black passage up to bed.

Farewell, O brother, sister, sire!
O pleasant party round the fire?
The songs you sing, the tales you tell,
Till far tomorrow, fare ye well!

2 SHADOW MARCH

All round the house is the jet-black night;
    It stares through the window-pane;
It crawls in the corners, hiding from the light,
    And it moves with the moving flame.

Now my little heart goes a-beating like a drum,
    With the breath of the Bogie in my hair;

And all round the candle the crooked shadows come
   And go marching along up the stair.

The shadow of the balusters, the shadow of the lamp,
   The shadow of the child that goes to bed –
All the wicked shadows coming, tramp, tramp, tramp,
   With the black night overhead.

3 IN PORT

Last, to the chamber where I lie
My fearful footsteps patter nigh,
And come from out the cold and gloom
Into my warm and cheerful room.

There, safe arrived, we turn about
To keep the coming shadows out,
And close the happy door at last
On all the perils that we past.

Then, when mamma goes by to bed,
She shall come in with tip-toe tread,
And see me lying warm and fast
And in the Land of Nod at last.

To My Name-Child

I

Some day soon this rhyming volume, if you learn with
    proper speed,
Little Louis Sanchez, will be given you to read.
Then shall you discover that your name was printed
    down
By the English printers, long before, in London town.

In the great and busy city where the East and West are
    met,
All the little letters did the English printer set;
While you thought of nothing, and were still too
    young to play,
Foreign people thought of you in places far away.

Ay, and while you slept, a baby, over all the English
    lands
Other little children took the volume in their hands;
Other children questioned, in their homes across the
    seas:
Who was little Louis, won't you tell us, mother,
    please?

2

Now that you have spelt your lesson, lay it down and
    go and play,
Seeking shells and seaweed on the sands of Monterey,
Watching all the mighty whalebones, lying buried by
    the breeze,
Tiny sandy-papers, and the huge Pacific seas.

And remember in your playing, as the sea-fog rolls to
   you,
Long ere you could read it, how I told you what to
   do;
And that while you thought of no one, nearly half the
   world away
Some one thought of Louis on the beach of Monterey!

To Any Reader

As from the house your mother sees
You playing round the garden trees,
So you may see, if you will look
Through the windows of this book,
Another child, far, far away,
And in another garden, play.
But do not think you can at all,
By knocking on the window, call
That child to hear you. He intent
Is all on his play-business bent.
He does not hear; he will not look,
Nor yet be lured out of this book.
For, long ago, the truth to say,
He has grown up and gone away,
And it is but a child of air
That lingers in the garden there.

from Ballads (1890)

from The Song of Rahéro
A Legend of Tahiti

2 THE VENGING OF TÁMATÉA

Thus was Rahéro's treason; thus and no further it sped.
The king sat safe in his place and a kindly fool was
   dead.

But the mother of Támatéa arose with death in her
   eyes.
All night long, and the next, Taiárapu rang with her
   cries.
As when a babe in the wood turns with a chill of
   doubt
And perceives nor home, nor friends, for the trees have
   closed her about,
The mountain rings and her breast is torn with the
   voice of despair:
So the lion-like woman idly wearied the air
For awhile, and pierced men's hearing in vain, and
   wounded their hearts.
But as when the weather changes at sea, in dangerous
   parts,
And sudden the hurricane wrack unrolls up the front of
   the sky,
At once the ship lies idle, the sails hang silent on high,
The breath of the wind that blew is blown out like the
   flame of a lamp,

And the silent armies of death draw near with
    inaudible tramp:
So sudden, the voice of her weeping ceased; in silence
    she rose
And passed from the house of her sorrow, a woman
    clothed with repose,
Carrying death in her breast and sharpening death with
    her hand.

Hither she went and thither in all the coasts of the
    land.
They tell that she feared not to slumber alone, in the
    dead of night,
In accursed places; beheld, unblenched, the ribbon of
    light
Spin from temple to temple; guided the perilous skiff,
Abhorred not the paths of the mountain and trod the
    verge of the cliff;
From end to end of the island, thought not the
    distance long,
But forth from king to king carried the tale of her
    wrong.
To king after king, as they sat in the palace door, she
    came,
Claiming kinship, declaiming verses, naming her name
And the names of all of her fathers; and still, with a
    heart on the rack,
Jested to capture a hearing and laughed when they
    jested back:
So would deceive them awhile, and change and return
    in a breath,
And on all the men of Vaiau imprecate instant death;
And tempt her kings – for Vaiau was a rich and
    prosperous land,

And flatter – for who would attempt it but warriors
  mighty of hand?
And change in a breath again and rise in a strain of
  song,
Invoking the beaten drums, beholding the fall of the
  strong,
Calling the fowls of the air to come and feast on the
  dead.
And they held the chin in silence, and heard her, and
  shook the head;
For they knew the men of Taiárapu famous in battle
  and feast,
Marvellous eaters and smiters: the man of Vaiau not
  least.

To the land of the Námunu-úra, to Paea, at length she
  came,
To men who were foes to the Tevas and hated their
  race and name,
There was she well received, and spoke with Hiopa the
  king.
And Hiopa listened, and weighed, and wisely
  considered the thing.
'Here in the back of the isle we dwell in a sheltered
  place,'
Quoth he to the woman, 'in quiet, a weak and
  peaceable race.
But far in the teeth of the wind lofty Taiárapu lies;
Strong blows the wind of the trade on its seaward face,
  and cries
Aloud in the top of arduous mountains, and utters its
  song
In green continuous forests. Strong is the wind, and
  strong

And fruitful and hardy the race, famous in battle and
  feast,
Marvellous eaters and smiters: the men of Vaiau not
  least.
Now hearken to me, my daughter, and hear a word of
  the wise:
How a strength goes linked with a weakness, two by
  two, like the eyes.
They can wield the ómare well and cast the javelin far;
Yet are they greedy and weak as the swine and the
  children are.
Plant we, then, here at Paea, a garden of excellent
  fruits;
Plant we bananas and kava and taro, the king of roots;
Let the pigs in Paea be tapu and no man fish for a
  year;
And of all the meat in Tahiti gather we threefold here.
So shall the fame of our plenty fill the island, and so,
At last, on the tongue of rumour, go where we wish it
  to go.
Then shall the pigs of Taiárapu raise their snouts in the
  air;
But we sit quiet and wait, as the fowler sits by the
  snare,
And tranquilly fold our hands, till the pigs come
  nosing the food:
But meanwhile build us a house of Trotéa, the
  stubborn wood,
Bind it with incombustible thongs, set a roof to the
  room,
Too strong for the hands of a man to dissever or fire
  to consume;
And there, when the pigs come trotting, there shall the
  feast be spread,

There shall the eye of the morn enlighten the feasters
    dead.
So be it done; for I have a heart that pities your state,
And Nateva and Námunu-úra are fire and water for
    hate.'

All was done as he said, and the gardens prospered;
    and now
The fame of their plenty went out, and word of it
    came to Vaiau.
For the men of Námunu-úra sailed, to the windward
    far,
Lay in the offing by south where the towns of the
    Tevas are,
And cast overboard of their plenty; and lo! at the
    Tevas' feet
The surf on all of the beaches tumbled treasures of
    meat.
In the salt of the sea, a harvest tossed with the refluent
    foam;
And the children gleaned it in playing, and ate and
    carried it home;
And the elders stared and debated, and wondered and
    passed the jest,
But whenever a guest came by eagerly questioned the
    guest;
And little by little, from one to another, the word
    went round:
'In all the borders of Paea the victual rots on the
    ground,
And swine are plenty as rats. And now, when they fare
    to the sea,
The men of the Námunu-úra glean from under the tree
And load the canoe to the gunwale with all that is
    toothsome to eat;

And all day long on the sea the jaws are crushing the
meat,
The steersman eats at the helm, the rowers munch at
the oar,
And at length, when their bellies are full, overboard
with the store!'
Now was the word made true, and soon as the bait
was bare,
All the pigs of Taiárapu raised their snouts in the air.
Songs were recited, and kinship was counted, and tales
were told
How war had severed of late but peace had cemented
of old
The clans of the island. 'To war,' said they, 'now set
we an end,
And hie to the Námunu-úra even as a friend to a
friend.'

So judged, and a day was named; and soon as the
morning broke,
Canoes were thrust in the sea and the houses emptied
of folk.
Strong blew the wind of the south, the wind that
gathers the clan;
Along all the line of the reef the clamorous surges ran;
And the clouds were piled on the top of the island
mountain-high,
A mountain throned on a mountain. The fleet of
canoes swept by
In the midst, on the green lagoon, with a crew
released from care,
Sailing an even water, breathing a summer air,
Cheered by a cloudless sun; and ever to left and right,

Bursting surge on the reef, drenching storms on the height.
So the folk of Vaiau sailed and were glad all day,
Coasting the palm-tree cape and crossing the populous bay
By all the towns of the Tevas; and still as they bowled along,
Boat would answer to boat with jest and laughter and song,
And the people of all the towns trooped to the sides of the sea
And gazed from under the hand or sprang aloft on the tree,
Hailing and cheering. Time failed them for more to do;
The holiday village careened to the wind, and was gone from view
Swift as a passing bird; and ever as onward it bore,
Like the cry of the passing bird, bequeathed its song to the shore –
Desirable laughter of maids and the cry of delight of the child.
And the gazer, left behind, stared at the wake and smiled.
By all the towns of the Tevas they went, and Pápara last,
The home of the chief, the place of muster in war; and passed
The march of the lands of the clan, to the lands of an alien folk.
And there, from the dusk of the shoreside palms, a column of smoke
Mounted and wavered and died in the gold of the setting sun,

'Paea!' they cried. 'It is Paea.' And so was the voyage done.

In the early fall of the night, Hiopa came to the shore,
And beheld and counted the comers, and lo, they were forty score:
The pelting feet of the babes that ran already and played,
The clean-lipped smile of the boy, the slender breasts of the maid,
And mighty limbs of women, stalwart mothers of men.
The sires stood forth unabashed; but a little back from his ken
Clustered the scarcely nubile, the lads and maids, in a ring,
Fain of each other, afraid of themselves, aware of the king
And aping behaviour, but clinging together with hands and eyes,
With looks that were kind like kisses, and laughter tender as sighs.
There, too, the grandsire stood, raising his silver crest,
And the impotent hands of a suckling groped in his barren breast.
The childhood of love, the pair well married, the innocent brood,
The tale of the generations repeated and ever renewed –
Hiopa beheld them together, all the ages of man,
And a moment shook in his purpose.

                          But these were the foes of his clan,
And he trod upon pity, and came, and civilly greeted the king,

And gravely entreated Rahéro; and for all that could
    fight or sing,
And claimed a name in the land, had fitting phrases of
    praise;
But with all who were well-descended he spoke of the
    ancient days.
And ''Tis true,' said he, 'that in Paea the victual rots
    on the ground;
But, friends, your number is many; and pigs must be
    hunted and found,
And the lads troop to the mountains to bring the féis
    down,
And around the bowls of the kava cluster the maids of
    the town.
So, for tonight, sleep here; but king, common, and
    priest
Tomorrow, in order due, shall sit with me in the
    feast.'
Sleepless the live-long night, Hiopa's followers toiled.
The pigs screamed and were slaughtered; the spars of
    the guest-house oiled,
The leaves spread on the floor. In many a mountain
    glen
The moon drew shadows of trees on the naked bodies
    of men
Plucking and bearing fruits; and in all the bounds of
    the town
Red glowed the cocoanut fires, and were buried and
    trodden down.
Thus did seven of the yottowas toil with their tale of
    the clan,
But the eighth wrought with his lads, hid from the
    sight of man.

In the deeps of the woods they laboured, piling the
    fuel high
In faggots, the load of man, fuel seasoned and dry,
Thirsty to seize upon fire and apt to blurt into flame.

And now was the day of the feast. The forests, as
    morning came,
Tossed in the wind, and the peaks quaked in the blaze
    of the day
And the cocoanuts showered on the ground,
    rebounding and rolling away:
A glorious morn for a feast, a famous wind for a fire.
To the hall of feasting Hiopa led them, mother and sire
And maid and babe in a tale, the whole of the holiday
    throng.
Smiling they came, garlanded green, not dreaming of
    wrong;
And for every three, a pig, tenderly cooked in the
    ground,
Waited; and féi, the staff of life, heaped in a mound
For each where he sat; – for each, bananas roasted and
    raw
Piled with a bountiful hand, as for horses hay and
    straw
Are stacked in a stable; and fish, the food of desire,
And plentiful vessels of sauce, and breadfruit gilt in the
    fire;
And kava was common as water. Feasts have there been
    ere now,
And many, but never a feast like that of the folk of
    Vaiau.
All day long they ate with the resolute greed of brutes,
And turned from the pigs to the fish, and again from
    the fish to the fruits,

And emptied the vessels of sauce, and drank of the
  kava deep;
Till the young lay stupid as stones, and the strongest
  nodded to sleep.
Sleep that was mighty as death and blind as a moonless
  night
Tethered them hand and foot; and their souls were
  drowned, and the light
Was cloaked from their eyes. Senseless together, the old
  and the young,
The fighter deadly to smite and the prater cunning of
  tongue,
The woman wedded and fruitful, inured to the pangs
  of birth,
And the maid that knew not of kisses, blindly sprawled
  on the earth.
From the hall Hiopa the king and his chiefs came
  stealthily forth.
Already the sun hung low and enlightened the peaks of
  the north;
But the wind was stubborn to die and blew as it blows
  at morn,
Showering the nuts in the dusk, and e'en as a banner
  is torn,
High on the peaks of the island, shattered the
  mountain cloud.
And now at once, at a signal, a silent, emulous crowd
Set hands to the work of death, hurrying to and fro,
Like ants, to furnish the faggots, building them broad
  ¯ and low,
And piling them high and higher around the walls of
  the hall.
Silence persisted within, for sleep lay heavy on all;
But the mother of Támatéa stood at Hiopa's side,

And shook for terror and joy like a girl that is a bride.
Night fell on the toilers, and first Hiopa the wise
Made the round of the house, visiting all with his eyes;
And all was piled to the eaves, and fuel blockaded the
      door;
And within, in the house beleaguered, slumbered the
      forty score.
Then was an aito dispatched and came with fire in his
      hand,
And Hiopa took it. – 'Within,' said he, 'is the life of a
      land;
And behold! I breathe on the coal, I breathe on the
      dales of the east,
And silence falls on forest and shore; the voice of the
      feast
Is quenched, and the smoke of cooking; the rooftree
      decays and falls
On the empty lodge, and the winds subvert deserted
      walls.'

Therewithal, to the fuel, he laid the glowing coal;
And the redness ran in the mass and burrowed within
      like a mole,
And copious smoke was conceived. But, as when a
      dam is to burst,
The water lips it and crosses in silver trickles at first,
And then, of a sudden, whelms and bears it away
      forthright:
So now, in a moment, the flame sprang and towered
      in the night,
And wrestled and roared in the wind, and high over
      house and tree,
Stood, like a streaming torch, enlightening land and
      sea.

But the mother of Támatéa threw her arms abroad,
'Pyre of my son's,' she shouted, 'debited vengeance of
  God,
Late, late, I behold you, yet I behold you at last,
And glory, beholding! For now are the days of my
  agony past,
The lust that famished my soul now eats and drinks its
  desire,
And they that encompassed my son shrivel alive in the
  fire.
Tenfold precious the vengeance that comes after
  lingering years!
Ye quenched the voice of my singer? – hark, in your
  dying ears,
The song of the conflagration! Ye left me a widow
  alone?
– Behold, the whole of your race consumes, sinew and
  bone
And torturing flesh together: man, mother, and maid
Heaped in a common shambles; and already, borne by
  the trade,
The smoke of your dissolution darkens the stars of
  night.'

Thus she spoke, and her stature grew in the people's
  sight.

3 RAHÉRO

Rahéro was there in the hall asleep: beside him his
  wife,
Comely, a mirthful woman, one that delighted in life;
And a girl that was ripe for marriage, shy and sly as a
  mouse;

And a boy, a climber of trees: all the hopes of his
house.
Unwary, with open hands, he slept in the midst of his
folk,
And dreamed that he heard a voice crying without, and
awoke,
Leaping blindly afoot like one from a dream that he
fears.
A hellish glow and clouds were about him; – it roared
in his ears
Like the sound of the cataract fall that plunges sudden
and steep;
And Rahéro swayed as he stood, and his reason was
still asleep.
Now the flame struck hard on the house, wind-
wielded, a fracturing blow,
And the end of the roof was burst and fell on the
sleepers below;
And the lofty hall, and the feast, and the prostrate
bodies of folk,
Shone red in his eyes a moment, and then were
swallowed of smoke.
In the mind of Rahéro clearness came; and he opened
his throat;
And as when a squall comes sudden, the straining sail
of a boat
Thunders aloud and bursts, so thundered the voice of
the man.
– 'The wind and the rain!' he shouted, the mustering
word of the clan,
And 'up!' and 'to arms, men of Vaiau!' But silence
replied,
Or only the voice of the gusts of the fire, and nothing
beside.

Rahéro stooped and groped. He handled his
    womankind,
But the fumes of the fire and the kava had quenched
    the life of their mind,
And they lay like pillars prone; and his hand
    encountered the boy,
And there sprang in the gloom of his soul a sudden
    lightning of joy.
'Him can I save!' he thought, 'if I were speedy
    enough.'
And he loosened the cloth from his loins, and
    swaddled the child in the stuff;
And about the strength of his neck he knotted the
    burden well.

There where the roof had fallen, it roared like the
    mouth of hell.
Thither Rahéro went, stumbling on senseless folk,
And grappled a post of the house, and began to climb
    in the smoke:
The last alive of Vaiau; and the son borne by the sire.
The post glowed in the grain with ulcers of eating fire,
And the fire bit to the blood and mangled his hands
    and thighs;
And the fumes sang in his head like wine and stung in
    his eyes;
And still he climbed, and came to the top, the place of
    proof,
And thrust a hand through the flame, and clambered
    alive on the roof.
But even as he did so, the wind, in a garment of
    flames and pain,

Wrapped him from head to heel; and the waistcloth
    parted in twain;
And the living fruit of his loins dropped in the fire
    below.

About the blazing feast-house clustered the eyes of the
    foe,
Watching, hand upon weapon, lest ever a soul should
    flee,
Shading the brow from the glare, straining the neck to
    see.
Only, to leeward, the flames in the wind swept far and
    wide,
And the forest sputtered on fire; and there might no
    man abide.
Thither Rahéro crept, and dropped from the burning
    eaves,
And crouching low to the ground, in a treble covert of
    leaves
And fire and volleying smoke, ran for the life of his
    soul
Unseen; and behind him under a furnace of ardent
    coal,
Cairned with a wonder of flame, and blotting the night
    with smoke,
Blazed and were smelted together the bones of all his
    folk.

He fled unguided at first; but hearing the breakers roar,
Thitherward shaped his way, and came at length to the
    shore.
Sound-limbed he was: dry-eyed; but smarted in every
    part;

And the mighty cage of his ribs heaved on his
    straining heart
With sorrow and rage. And 'Fools!' he cried, 'fools of
    Vaiau,
Heads of swine – gluttons – Alas! and where are they
    now?
Those that I played with, those that nursed me, those
    that I nursed?
God, and I outliving them! I, the least and the worst –
I, that thought myself crafty; snared by this herd of
    swine,
In the tortures of hell and desolate, stripped of all that
    was mine:
All! – my friends and my fathers – the silver heads of
    yore
That trooped to the council, the children that ran to
    the open door
Crying with innocent voices and clasping a father's
    knees!
And mine, my wife – my daughter – my sturdy
    climber of trees,
Ah, never to climb again!'
                        Thus in the dusk of the night
(For clouds rolled in the sky and the moon was
    swallowed from sight),
Pacing and gnawing his fists, Rahéro raged by the
    shore.
Vengeance: that must be his. But much was to do
    before;
And first a single life to be snatched from a deadly
    place,
A life, the root of revenge, surviving plant of the race:
And next the race to be raised anew, and the lands of
    the clan

Repeopled. So Rahéro designed, a prudent man
Even in wrath, and turned for the means of revenge
    and escape:
A boat to be seized by stealth, a wife to be taken by
    rape.

Still was the dark lagoon; beyond on the coral wall,
He saw the breakers shine, he heard them bellow and
    fall.
Alone, on the top of the reef, a man with a flaming
    brand
Walked, gazing and pausing, a fish-spear poised in his
    hand.
The foam boiled to his calf when the mightier breakers
    came,
And the torch shed in the wind scattering tufts of
    flame.
Afar on the dark lagoon a canoe lay idly at wait:
A figure dimly guiding it: surely the fisherman's mate.
Rahéro saw and he smiled. He straightened his mighty
    thews:
Naked, with never a weapon, and covered with scorch
    and bruise,
He straightened his arms, he filled the void of his body
    with breath,
And, strong as the wind in his manhood, doomed the
    fisher to death.
Silent he entered the water, and silently swam, and came
There where the fisher walked, holding on high the
    flame.
Loud on the pier of the reef volleyed the breach of the
    sea;
And hard at the back of the man, Rahéro crept to his
    knee

On the coral, and suddenly sprang and seized him, the
  elder hand
Clutching the joint of his throat, the other snatching
  the brand
Ere it had time to fall, and holding it steady and high.
Strong was the fisher, brave, and swift of mind and of
  eye –
Strongly he threw in the clutch; but Rahéro resisted the
  strain,
And jerked, and the spine of life snapped with a crack
  in twain,
And the man came slack in his hands and tumbled a
  lump at his feet.

One moment: and there, on the reef, where the
  breakers whitened and beat,
Rahéro was standing alone, glowing and scorched and
  bare,
A victor unknown of any, raising the torch in the air.
But once he drank of his breath, and instantly set him
  to fish
Like a man intent upon supper at home and a savoury
  dish.
For what should the woman have seen? A man with a
  torch – and then
A moment's blur of the eyes – and a man with a torch
  again.
And the torch had scarcely been shaken. 'Ah, surely,'
  Rahéro said,
'She will deem it a trick of the eyes, a fancy born in
  the head;
But time must be given the fool to nourish a fool's
  belief.'

So for a while, a sedulous fisher, he walked the reef,
Pausing at times and gazing, striking at times with the
    spear:
– Lastly, uttered the call; and even as the boat drew
    near;
Like a man that was done with its use, tossed the torch
    in the sea.

Lightly he leaped on the boat beside the woman; and
    she
Lightly addressed him, and yielded the paddle and
    place to sit;
For now the torch was extinguished the night was
    black as the pit.
Rahéro set him to row, never a word he spoke,
And the boat sang in the water urged by his vigorous
    stroke.
– 'What ails you?' the woman asked, 'and why did
    you drop the brand?'
We have only to kindle another as soon as we come to
    land.'
Never a word Rahéro replied, but urged the canoe.
And a chill fell on the woman. – 'Atta! speak! is it
    you?
Speak! Why are you silent? Why do you bend aside?
Wherefore steer to the seaward?' thus she panted and
    cried.
Never a word from the oarsman, toiling there in the
    dark;
But right for a gate of the reef he silently headed the
    bark,
And wielding the single paddle with passionate sweep
    on sweep,
Drove her, the little fitted, forth on the open deep.

And fear, there where she sat, froze the woman to
    stone:
Not fear of the crazy boat and the weltering deep
    alone;
But a keener fear of the night, the dark, and the
    ghostly hour,
And the thing that drove the canoe with more than a
    mortal's power
And more than a mortal's boldness. For much she
    knew of the dead
That haunt and fish upon reefs, toiling, like men, for
    bread,
And traffic with human fishers, or slay them and take
    their ware,
Till the hour when the star of the dead goes down,
    and the morning air
Blows, and the cocks are singing on shore. And surely
    she knew
The speechless thing at her side belonged to the grave.
                                                It blew
All night from the south; all night, Rahéro contended
    and kept
The prow to the cresting sea; and, silent as though she
    slept,
The woman huddled and quaked. And now was the
    peep of day.
High and long on their left the mountainous island lay;
And over the peaks of Taiárapu arrows of sunlight
    struck.
On shore the birds were beginning to sing: the ghostly
    ruck
Of the buried had long ago returned to the covered
    grave;

And here on the sea, the woman, waxing suddenly
    brave,
Turned her swiftly about and looked in the face of the
    man.
And sure he was none that she knew, none of her
    country or clan:
A stranger, mother-naked, and marred with the marks
    of fire,
But comely and great of stature, a man to obey and
    admire.
And Rahéro regarded her also, fixed, with a frowning
    face,
Judging the woman's fitness to mother a warlike race.
Broad of shoulder, ample of girdle, long in the thigh,
Deep of bosom she was, and bravely supported his eye.

'Woman,' said he, 'last night the men of your folk –
Man, woman, and maid, smothered my race in smoke.
It was done like cowards; and I, a mighty man of my
    hands,
Escaped, a single life; and now to the empty lands
And smokeless hearths of my people, sail, with
    yourself, alone.
Before your mother was born, the die of today was
    thrown
And you selected: – your husband, vainly striving, to
    fall
Broken between these hands: – yourself to be severed
    from all,
The places, the people, you love – home, kindred, and
    clan –
And to dwell in a desert and bear the babes of a
    kinless man.'

Heather Ale
A Galloway Legend

From the bonny bells of heather
   They brewed a drink long-syne,
Was sweeter far than honey,
   Was stronger far than wine.
They brewed it and they drank it,
   And lay in a blessed swound
For days and days together
   In their dwellings underground.

There rose a king in Scotland,
   A fell man to his foes,
He smote the Picts in battle,
   He hunted them like roes.
Over miles of the red mountain
   He hunted as they fled,
And strewed the dwarfish bodies
   Of the dying and the dead.

Summer came in the country,
   Red was the heather bell;
But the manner of the brewing
   Was none alive to tell.
In graves that were like children's
   On many a mountain's head,
The Brewsters of the Heather
   Lay numbered with the dead.

The king in the red moorland
   Rode on a summer's day;
And the bees hummed, and the curlews

Cried beside the way.
The king rode, and was angry,
　　Black was his brow and pale,
To rule in a land of heather
　　And lack the Heather Ale.

It fortuned that his vassals,
　　Riding free on the heath,
Came on a stone that was fallen
　　And vermin hid beneath.
Rudely plucked from their hiding,
　　Never a word they spoke:
A son and his aged father –
　　Last of the dwarfish folk.

The king sat high on his charger,
　　He looked on the little men;
And the dwarfish and swarthy couple
　　Looked at the king again.
Down by the shore he had them:
　　And there on the giddy brink –
'I will give you life, ye vermin,
　　For the secret of the drink.'

There stood the son and father
　　And they looked high and low;
The heather was red around them,
　　The sea rumbled below.
And up and spoke the father,
　　Shrill was his voice to hear:
'I have a word in private,
　　A word for the royal ear.

'Life is dear to the aged,
    And honour a little thing;
I would gladly sell the secret,'
    Quoth the Pict to the King.
His voice was small as a sparrow's,
    And shrill and wonderful clear:
'I would gladly sell my secret,
    Only my son I fear.

'For life is a little matter,
    And death is nought to the young;
And I dare not sell my honour
    Under the eye of my son.
Take him, O king, and bind him,
    And cast him far in the deep;
And it's I will tell the secret
    That I have sworn to keep.'

They took the son and bound him,
    Neck and heels in a thong,
And a lad took him and swung him,
    And flung him far and strong,
And the sea swallowed his body,
    Like that of a child of ten;
And there on the cliff stood the father,
    Last of the dwarfish men.

'True was the word I told you:
    Only my son I feared;
For I doubt the sapling courage
    That goes without the beard.
But now in vain is the torture,
    Fire shall never avail:
Here dies in my bosom
    The secret of Heather Ale.'

from Songs of Travel (1895)

The Vagabond

To an air of Schubert

Give to me the life I love,
   Let the lave go by me,
Give the jolly heaven above
   And the byway nigh me.
Bed in the bush with stars to see,
   Bread I dip in the river –
There's the life for a man like me;
   There's the life for ever.

Let the blow fall soon or late,
   Let what will be o'er me;
Give the face of earth around
   And the road before me.
Wealth I seek not, hope nor love,
   Nor a friend to know me;
All I seek, the heaven above
   And the road below me.

Or let autumn fall on me
   Where afield I linger,
Silencing the bird on tree,
   Biting the blue finger.
White as meal the frosty field –
   Warm the fireside haven –
Not to autumn will I yield,
   Not to winter even!

Let the blow fall soon or late,
    Let what will be o'er me;
Give the face of earth around,
    And the road before me.
Wealth I ask not, hope nor love,
    Nor a friend to know me;
All I ask the heaven above,
    And the road below me.

I will make you brooches . . .

I will make you brooches and toys for your delight
Of bird-song at morning and star-shine at night.
I will make a palace fit for you and me
Of green days in forests and blue days at sea.

I will make my kitchen, and you shall keep your room,
Where white flows the river and bright blows the broom,
And you shall wash your linen and keep your body white
In rainfall at morning and dewfall at night.

And this shall be for music when no one else is near,
The fine song for singing, the rare song to hear!
That only I remember, that only you admire,
Of the broad road that stretches and the roadside fire.

Bright is the ring of words . . .

Bright is the ring of words
    When the right man rings them,
Fair the fall of songs
    When the singer sings them.
Still they are carolled and said –
    On wings they are carried –
After the singer is dead
    And the maker buried.

Low as the singer lies
    In the field of heather,
Songs of his fashion bring
    The swains together.
And when the west is red
    With the sunset embers,
The lover lingers and sings
    And the maid remembers.

In the highlands, in the country places . . .

In the highlands, in the country places,
Where the old plain men have rosy faces,
And the young fair maidens
Quiet eyes;
Where essential silence cheers and blesses,
And for ever in the hill-recesses
Her more lovely music
Broods and dies.

O to mount again where erst I haunted;
Where the old red hills are bird-enchanted,
And the low green meadows
Bright with sward;
And when even dies, the million-tinted,
And the night has come, and planets glinted,
Lo, the valley hollow
Lamp-bestarred!

O to dream, O to awake and wander
There, and with delight to take and render,
Through the trance of silence,
Quiet breath;
Lo! for there, among the flowers and grasses,
Only the mightier movement sounds and passes;
Only winds and rivers,
Life and death.

To the Tune of Wandering Willie

Home no more home to me, whither must I wander?
  Hunger my driver, I go where I must.
Cold blows the winter wind over hill and heather;
  Thick drives the rain, and my roof is in the dust.
Loved of wise men was the shade of my roof-tree.
  The true word of welcome was spoken in the door –
Dear days of old, with the faces in the firelight,
  Kind folks of old, you come again no more.

Home was home then, my dear, full of kindly faces,
  Home was home then, my dear, happy for the child.
Fire and the windows bright glittered on the moorland;
  Song, tuneful song, built a palace in the wild.
Now, when day dawns on the brow of the moorland,
  Lone stands the house, and the chimney-stone is cold.
Lone let it stand, now the friends are all departed,
  The kind hearts, the true hearts, that loved the place
    of old.

Spring shall come, come again, calling up the
    moorfowl,
  Spring shall bring the sun and rain, bring the bees
    and flowers;
Red shall the heather bloom over hill and valley,
  Soft flow the stream through the even-flowing hours;
Fair the day shine as it shone on my childhood –
  Fair shine the day on the house with open door;
Birds come and cry there and twitter in the chimney –
  But I go for ever and come again no more.

My Wife

Trusty, dusky, vivid, true,
With eyes of gold and bramble-dew,
Steel-true and blade-straight,
The great artificer
Made my mate.

Honour, anger, valour, fire;
A love that life could never tire,
Death quench or evil stir,
The mighty master
Gave to her.

Teacher, tender comrade, wife,
A fellow-farer true through life,
Heart-whole and soul-free
The august father
Gave to me.

To an Island Princess

Since long ago, a child at home,
I read and longed to rise and roam,
Where'er I went, whate'er I willed,
One promised land my fancy filled.
Hence the long roads my home I made;
Tossed much in ships; have often laid
Below the uncurtained sky my head,
Rain-deluged and wind-buffeted:
And many a thousand hills I crossed
And corners turned – Love's labour lost,
Till, Lady, to your isle of sun
I came, not hoping; and, like one
Snatched out of blindness, rubbed my eyes,
And hailed my promised land with cries.

Yes, Lady, here I was at last;
Here found I all I had forecast:
The long roll of the sapphire sea
That keeps the land's virginity;
The stalwart giants of the wood
Laden with toys and flowers and food;
The precious forest pouring out
To compass the whole town about;
The town itself with streets of lawn,
Loved of the moon, blessed by the dawn,
Where the brown children all the day
Keep up a ceaseless noise of play,
Play in the sun, play in the rain,
Nor ever quarrel or complain;
And late at night, in the woods of fruit,
Hark! do you hear the passing flute?

I threw one look to either hand,
And knew I was in Fairyland.
And yet one point of being so,
I lacked. For, Lady (as you know),
Whoever by his might of hand,
Won entrance into Fairyland,
Found always with admiring eyes
A Fairy princess kind and wise.
It was not long I waited; soon
Upon my threshold, in broad noon,
Gracious and helpful, wise and good,
The Fairy Princess Moë stood.

To Kalakaua

With a present of a Pearl

The Silver Ship, my King – that was her name
In the bright islands whence your fathers came –
The Silver Ship, at rest from winds and tides,
Below your palace in your harbour rides:
And the seafarers, sitting safe on shore,
Like eager merchants count their treasure o'er.
One gift they find, one strange and lovely thing,
Now doubly precious since it pleased a king.

The right, my liege, is ancient as the lyre
For bards to give to kings what kings admire.
'Tis mine to offer for Apollo's sake;
And since the gift is fitting, yours to take.
To golden hands the golden pearl I bring:
The ocean jewel to the island king.

To Princess Kaiulani

Forth from her land to mine she goes,
The island maid, the island rose,
Light of heart and bright of face:
The daughter of a double race.

Her islands here, in Southern sun,
Shall mourn their Kaiulani gone,
And I, in her dear banyan shade,
Look vainly for my little maid.

But our Scots islands far away
Shall glitter with unwonted day,
And cast for once their tempests by
To smile in Kaiulani's eye.

To My Old Familiars

Do you remember – can we e'er forget? –
How, in the coiled perplexities of youth,
In our wild climate, in our scowling town,
We gloomed and shivered, sorrowed, sobbed and
  feared?
The belching winter wind, the missile rain,
The rare and welcome silence of the snows,
The laggard morn, the haggard day, the night,
The grimy spell of the nocturnal town,
Do you remember? – Ah, could one forget!

As when the fevered sick that all night long
Listed the wind intone, and hear at last
The ever-welcome voice of chanticleer
Sing in the bitter hour before the dawn,
With sudden ardour, these desire the day:
So sang in the gloom of youth the bird of hope;
So we, exulting, hearkened and desired.
For lo! as in the palace porch of life
We huddled with chimeras, from within –
How sweet to hear! – the music swelled and fell,
And through the breach of the revolving doors
What dreams of splendour blinded us and fled!

I have since then contended and rejoiced;
Amid the glories of the house of life
Profoundly entered, and the shrine beheld:
Yet when the lamp from my expiring eyes
Shall dwindle and recede, the voice of love
Fall insignificant on my closing ears,
What sound shall come but the old cry of the wind

In our inclement city? what return
But the image of the emptiness of youth,
Filled with the sound of footsteps and that voice
Of discontent and rapture and despair?
So, as in darkness, from the magic lamp,
The momentary pictures gleam and fade
And perish, and the night resurges – these
Shall I remember, and then all forget.

The tropics vanish . . .

The tropics vanish, and meseems that I,
From Halkerside, from topmost Allermuir,
Or steep Caerketton, dreaming gaze again.
Far set in fields and woods, the town I see
Spring gallant from the shallows of her smoke,
Cragged, spired, and turreted, her virgin fort
Beflagged. About, on seaward-drooping hills,
New folds of city glitter. Last, the Forth
Wheels ample waters set with sacred isles,
And populous Fife smokes with a score of towns.

There, on the sunny frontage of a hill,
Hard by the house of kings, repose the dead,
My dead, the ready and the strong of word.
Their works, the salt-encrusted, still survive;
The sea bombards their founded towers; the night
Thrills pierced with their strong lamps. The artificers,
One after one, here in this grated cell,
Where the rain erases and the rust consumes,
Fell upon lasting silence. Continents
And continental oceans intervene;
A sea uncharted, on a lampless isle,
Environs and confines their wandering child
In vain. The voice of generations dead
Summons me, sitting distant, to arise,
My numerous footsteps nimbly to retrace,
And, all mutation over, stretch me down
In that devoted city of the dead.

To S. C.

I heard the pulse of the besieging sea
Throb far away all night. I heard the wind
Fly crying and convulse tumultuous palms.
I rose and strolled. The isle was all bright sand,
And flailing fans and shadows of the palm;
The heaven all moon and wind and the blind vault;
The keenest planet slain, for Venus slept.

The king, my neighbour, with his host of wives,
Slept in the precinct of the palisade;
Where single, in the wind, under the moon,
Among the slumbering cabins, blazed a fire,
Sole street-lamp and the only sentinel.

To other lands and nights my fancy turned –
To London first, and chiefly to your house,
The many-pillared and the well-beloved.
There yearning fancy lighted; there again
In the upper room I lay, and heard far off
The unsleeping city murmur like a shell;
The muffled tramp of the Museum guard
Once more went by me; I beheld again
Lamps vainly brighten the dispeopled street;
Again I longed for the returning morn,
The awaking traffic, the bestirring birds,
The consentaneous trill of tiny song
That weaves round monumental cornices
A passing charm of beauty. Most of all,
For your light foot I wearied, and your knock
That was the glad réveillé of my day.

Lo, now, when to your task in the great house
At morning through the portico you pass,
One moment glance, where by the pillared wall

Far-voyaging island gods, begrimmed with smoke,
Sit now unworshipped, the rude monument
Of faiths forgot and races undivined:
Sit now disconsolate, remembering well
The priest, the victim, and the songful crowd,
The blaze of the blue noon, and the huge voice,
Incessant, of the breakers on the shore.
As far as these from their ancestral shrine,
So far, so foreign, your divided friends
Wander, estranged in body, not in mind.

The Woodman

In all the grove, nor stream nor bird
Nor aught beside my blows was heard,
And the woods wore their noonday dress –
The glory of their silentness.
From the island summit to the seas,
Trees mounted, and trees drooped, and trees
Groped upward in the gaps. The green
Inarboured talus and ravine
By fathoms. By the multitude,
The rugged columns of the wood
And bunches of the branches stood;
Thick as a mob, deep as a sea,
And silent as eternity.

With lowered axe, with backward head,
Late from this scene my labourer fled,
And with a ravelled tale to tell,
Returned. Some denizen of hell,
Dead man or disinvested god,
Had close behind him peered and trod,
And triumphed when he turned to flee.
How different fell the lines with me!
Whose eye explored the dim arcade
Impatient of the uncoming shade –
Shy elf, or dryad pale and cold,
Or mystic lingerer from of old:
Vainly. The fair and stately things,
Impassive as departed kings,
All still in the wood's stillness stood,
And dumb. The rooted multitude
Nodded and brooded, bloomed and dreamed,

Unmeaning, undivined. It seemed
No other art, no hope, they knew,
Than clutch the earth and seek the blue.
Mid vegetable king and priest
And stripling, I (the only beast)
Was at the beast's work, killing; hewed
The stubborn roots across, bestrewed
The glebe with the dislustred leaves,
And bade the saplings fall in sheaves;
Bursting across the tangled math
A ruin that I called a path,
A Golgotha that, later on,
When rains had watered, and suns shone,
And seeds enriched the place, should bear
And be called garden. Here and there,
I spied and plucked by the green hair
A foe more resolute to live,
The toothed and killing sensitive.
He, semi-conscious, fled the attack;
He shrank and tucked his branches back;
And straining by his anchor-strand,
Captured and scratched the rooting hand.
I saw him crouch, I felt him bite;
And straight my eyes were touched with sight.
I saw the wood for what it was:
The lost and the victorious cause,
The deadly battle pitched in line,
Saw silent weapons cross and shine:
Silent defeat, silent assault,
A battle and a burial vault.

Thick round me in the teeming mud
Briar and fern strove to the blood:
The hooked liana in his gin

Noosed his reluctant neighbours in:
There the green murderer throve and spread,
Upon his smothering victims fed,
And wantoned on his climbing coil.
Contending roots fought for the soil
Like frightened demons: with despair
Competing branches pushed for air.
Green conquerors from overhead
Bestrode the bodies of their dead:
The Caesars of the sylvan field,
Unused to fail, foredoomed to yield:
For in the groins of branches, lo!
The cancers of the orchid grow.
Silent as in the listed ring
Two chartered wrestlers strain and cling;
Dumb as by yellow Hooghly's side
The suffocating captives died;
So hushed the woodland warfare goes
Unceasing; and the silent foes
Grapple and smother, strain and clasp
Without a cry, without a gasp.
Here also sound thy fans, O God,
Here too thy banners move abroad:
Forest and city, sea and shore,
And the whole earth, thy threshing-floor!
The drums of war, the drums of peace,
Roll through our cities without cease,
And all the iron halls of life
Ring with the unremitting strife.

The common lot we scarce perceive.
Crowds perish, we nor mark nor grieve:
The bugle calls – we mourn a few!
What corporal's guard at Waterloo?

What scanty hundreds more or less
In the man-devouring Wilderness?
What handful bled on Delhi ridge?
– See, rather, London, on thy bridge
The pale battalions trample by,
Resolved to slay, resigned to die.
Count, rather, all the maimed and dead
In the unbrotherly war of bread.
See, rather, under sultrier skies
What vegetable Londons rise,
And teem, and suffer without sound:
Or in your tranquil garden ground,
Contented, in the falling gloom,
Saunter and see the roses bloom.
That these might live, what thousands died!
All day the cruel hoe was plied;
The ambulance barrow rolled all day;
Your wife, the tender, kind, and gay,
Donned her long gauntlets, caught the spud,
And bathed in vegetable blood;
And the long massacre now at end,
See! where the lazy coils ascend,
See, where the bonfire sputters red
At even, for the innocent dead.

Why prate of peace? when, warriors all,
We clank in harness into hall,
And ever bare upon the board
Lies the necessary sword.
In the green field or quiet street,
Besieged we sleep, beleaguered eat;
Labour by day and wake o' nights,
In war with rival appetites.
The rose on roses feeds; the lark

On larks. The sedentary clerk
All morning with a diligent pen
Murders the babes of other men;
And like the beasts of wood and park,
Protects his whelps, defends his den.

Unshamed the narrow aim I hold;
I feed my sheep, patrol my fold;
Breathe war on wolves and rival flocks,
A pious outlaw on the rocks
Of God and morning; and when time
Shall bow, or rivals break me, climb
Where no undubbed civilian dares,
In my war harness, the loud stairs
Of honour; and my conqueror
Hail me a warrior fallen in war.

Tropic Rain

As the single pang of the blow, when the metal is
  mingled well,
Rings and lives and resounds in all the bounds of the
  bell,
So the thunder above spoke with a single tongue,
So in the heart of the mountain the sound of it
  rumbled and clung.
Sudden the thunder was drowned – quenched was the
  levin light –
And the angle-spirit of rain laughed out loud in the
  night.
Loud as the maddened river raves in the cloven glen,
Angel of rain! you laughed and leaped on the roofs of
  men;
And the sleepers sprang in their beds, and joyed and
  feared as you fell.
You struck, and my cabin quailed; the roof of it roared
  like a bell,
You spoke, and at once the mountain shouted and
  shook with brooks.
You ceased, and the day returned, rosy, with virgin
  looks.

And methought that beauty and terror are only one,
  not two;
And the world has room for love, and death, and
  thunder, and dew;
And all the sinews of hell slumber in summer air;
And the face of God is a rock, but the face of the rock
  is fair.

Beneficent streams of tears flow at the finger of pain;
And out of the cloud that smites, beneficent rivers of
rain.

The Last Sight

Once more I saw him. In the lofty room,
Where oft with lights and company his tongue
Was trump to honest laughter, sate attired
A something in his likeness. 'Look!' said one,
Unkindly kind, 'look up, it is your boy!'
And the dread changeling gazed on me in vain.

Sing me a song of a lad that is gone . . .

Sing me a song of a lad that is gone,
  Say, could that lad be I?
Merry of soul he sailed on a day
  Over the sea to Skye.

Mull was astern, Rum on the port,
  Eigg on the starboard bow;
Glory of youth glowed in his soul;
  Where is that glory now?

Sing me a song of a lad that is gone,
  Say, could that lad be I?
Merry of soul he sailed on a day
  Over the sea to Skye.

Give me again all that was there,
  Give me the sun that shone!
Give me the eyes, give me the soul,
  Give me the lad that's gone!

Sing me a song of a lad that is gone,
  Say, could that lad be I?
Merry of soul he sailed on a day
  Over the sea to Skye.

Billow and breeze, islands and seas,
  Mountains of rain and sun,
All that was good, all that was fair,
  All that was me is gone.

To S. R. Crockett

On receiving a Dedication

Blows the wind today, and the sun and the rain are
      flying,
  Blows the wind on the moors today and now,
Where about the graves of the martyrs the whaups are
      crying,
  My heart remembers how!

Grey recumbent tombs of the dead in desert places,
  Standing-stones on the vacant wine-red moor,
Hills of sheep, and the howes of the silent vanished
      races,
  And winds, austere and pure.

Be it granted me to behold you again in dying,
  Hills of home! and to hear again the call;
Hear about the graves of the martyrs the peewees
      crying,
  And hear no more at all.

Poems first published in fiction and later poems published posthumously

Robin and Ben: or, the Pirate and the Apothecary

Come lend me an attentive ear
A startling moral tale to hear,
Of Pirate Rob and Chemist Ben,
And different destinies of men.

Deep in the greenest of the vales
That nestle near the coast of Wales,
The heaving main but just in view,
Robin and Ben together grew,
Together worked and played the fool,
Together shunned the Sunday school,
And pulled each other's youthful noses
Around the cots, among the roses.

Together but unlike they grew;
Robin was rough, and through and through,
Bold, inconsiderable, and manly,
Like some historic Bruce or Stanley.
Ben had a mean and servile soul,
He robbed not, though he often stole.
He sang on Sunday in the choir,
And tamely capped the passing Squire.

At length, intolerant of trammels —
Wild as the wild Bithynian camels,
Wild as the wild sea-eagles — Bob
His widowed dam contrives to rob,
And thus with great originality
Effectuates his personality.
Thenceforth his terror-haunted flight
He follows through the starry night;
And with the early morning breeze,
Behold him on the azure seas.
The master of a trading dandy
Hires Robin for a go of brandy;
And all the happy hills of home
Vanish beyond the fields of foam.

Ben, meanwhile, like a tin reflector,
Attended on the worthy rector;
Opened his eyes and held his breath,
And flattered to the point of death;
And was at last, by that good fairy,
Apprenticed to the Apothecary.

So, Ben, while Robin chose to roam,
A rising chemist was at home,
Tended his shop with learnèd air,
Watered his drugs and oiled his hair,
And gave advice to the unwary,
Like any sleek apothecary.

Meanwhile upon the deep afar
Robin the brave was waging war,
With other tarry desperadoes
About the latitude of Barbadoes.
He knew no touch of craven fear;

His voice was thunder in the cheer;
First, from the main-to'-gallan' high,
The skulking merchantman to spy –
The first to bound upon the deck,
The last to leave the sinking wreck.
His hand was steel, his word was law,
His mates regarded him with awe.
No pirate in the whole profession
Held a more honourable position.

At length, from years of anxious toil,
Bold Robin seeks his native soil;
Wisely arranges his affairs,
And to his native dale repairs.
The Bristol *Swallow* sets him down
Beside the well-remembered town.
He sighs, he spits, he marks the scene,
Proudly he treads the village green;
And free from pettiness and rancour,
Takes lodgings at the 'Crown and Anchor'.

Strange, when a man so great and good,
Once more in his home-country stood,
Strange that the sordid clowns should show
A dull desire to have him go.
His clinging breeks, his tarry hat,
The way he swore, the way he spat,
A certain quality of manner,
Alarming like the pirate's banner –
Something that did not seem to suit all –
Something, O call it bluff, not brutal –
Something at least, howe'er it's called,
Made Robin generally black-balled.

His soul was wounded; proud and glum,
Alone he sat and swigged his rum,
And took a great distaste to men
Till he encountered Chemist Ben.
Bright was the hour and bright the day,
That threw them in each other's way;
Glad were their mutual salutations,
Long their respective revelations.
Before the inn in sultry weather
They talked of this and that together;
Ben told the tale of his indentures,
And Rob narrated his adventures.
Last, as the point of greatest weight,
The pair contrasted their estate,
And Robin, like a boastful sailor,
Despised the other for a tailor.

'See,' he remarked, 'with envy, see
A man with such a fist as me!
Bearded and ringed, and big, and brown,
I sit and toss the stingo down,
Hear the gold jingle in my bag –
All won beneath the Jolly Flag!'

Ben moralised and shook his head:
'You wanderers earn and eat your bread.
The foe is found, beats or is beaten,
And either how, the wage is eaten.
And after all your pully-hauly
Your proceeds look uncommon small-ly.
You had done better here to tarry
Apprentice to the Apothecary.
The silent pirates of the shore
Eat and sleep soft, and pocket more

Than any red, robustious ranger
Who picks his farthings hot from danger.
You clank your guineas on the board;
Mine are with several bankers stored.
You reckon riches on your digits,
You dash in chase of Sals and Bridgets,
You drink and risk delirium tremens,
Your whole estate a common seaman's!
Regard your friend and school companion,
Soon to be wed to Miss Trevanion
(Smooth, honourable, fat and flowery,
With Heaven knows how much land in dowry),
Look at me – am I in good case?
Look at my hands, look at my face;
Look at the cloth of my apparel;
Try me and test me, lock and barrel;
And own, to give the devil his due,
I have made more of life than you.
Yet I nor sought nor risked a life;
I shudder at an open knife;
The perilous seas I still avoided
And stuck to land whate'er betided.
I had no gold, no marble quarry,
I was a poor apothecary,
Yet here I stand, at thirty-eight,
A man of an assured estate.'

'Well,' answered Robin – 'well, and how?'

The smiling chemist tapped his brow.
'Rob,' he replied, 'this throbbing brain
Still worked and hankered after gain.
By day and night, to work my will,
It pounded like a powder mill;

And marking how the world went round
A theory of theft it found.
Here is the key to right and wrong:
Steal little, but steal all day long;
And this invaluable plan
Marks what is called the Honest Man.
When first I served with Doctor Pill,
My hand was ever in the till.
Now that I am myself a master
My gains come softer still and faster.
As thus: on Wednesday, a maid
Came to me in the way of trade.
Her mother, an old farmer's wife,
Required a drug to save her life.
'At once, my dear, at once,' I said,
Patted the child upon the head,
Bade her be still a loving daughter,
And filled the bottle up with water.'

'Well, and the mother?' Robin cried.

'O she!' said Ben, 'I think she died.'

'Battle and blood, death and disease,
Upon the tainted Tropic seas –
The attendant sharks that chew the cud –
The abhorred scuppers spouting blood –
The untended dead, the Tropic sun –
The thunder of the murderous gun –
The cut-throat crew – the Captain's curse –
The tempest blustering worse and worse –
These have I known and these can stand,
But you, I settle out of hand!'

Out flashed the cutlass, down went Ben
Dead and rotten, there and then.

Translations From Martial:
In Lupum
XI. 18

Beyond the gates, you gave a farm to till:
I have a larger on my window-sill!
A farm, d'ye say? Is this a farm to you? –
Where for all woods I spy one tuft of rue,
And that so rusty, and so small a thing,
One shrill cicada hides it with a wing;
Where one cucumber covers all the plain;
And where one serpent rings himself in vain
To enter wholly; and a single snail
Eats all, and exit fasting – to the jail,
Here shall I wait in vain till figs be set,
Or till the spring disclose the violet.
Through all my wilds a tameless mouse careers,
And in that narrow boundary appears,
Huge as the stalking lion of Algiers,
Huge as the fabled boar of Calydon.
And all my hay is at one swoop impresst.
By one low-flying swallow for her nest.
Strip god Priapus of each attribute
Here finds he scarce a pedestal to foot.
The gathered harvest scarcely brims a spoon;
And all my vintage drips in a cocoon.
Generous are you, but I more generous still:
Take back your farm and hand me half a gill!

In Charidemum

XI. 39

You, Charidemus, who my cradle swung
And watched me all the days that I was young –
You, at whose steps the laziest slaves awake
And both the bailiff and the butler quake –
The barber's suds now blacken with my beard
And my rough kisses make the maids afeard:
Still, in your eyes, before your judgement seat,
I am the baby that you used to beat.
You must do all things, unreproved; but I
If once to play or to my love I fly,
Big with reproach, I see your eyebrows twitch,
And for the accustomed cane your fingers itch.
If something daintily attired I go,
Straight you exclaim: 'Your father did not so!'
And, frowning, count the bottles on the board,
As though my cellar were your private hoard.
Enough, at last! I have borne all I can,
And your own mistress hails me for a man.

If I could arise and travel away . . .

If I could arise and travel away
Over the plains of the night and the day,
I should arrive at a land at last
Where all of our sins and sorrows are past
   And we're done with the ten commandments.

The name of the land I must not tell;
Green is the grass and cool the well;
Virtue is easy to find and to keep,
And the sinner may lie at his pleasure and sleep
   By the side of the ten commandments.

Income and honour, and glory and gold
Grow on the bushes all over the wold;
And if ever a man has a touch of remorse,
He eats of the flower of the golden gorse,
   And to hell with the ten commandments.

He goes to church in his Sunday's best;
He eats and drinks with perfect zest;
And whether he lives in heaven or hell
Is more than you or I can tell;
   But he's done with the ten commandments.

To the Hesitating Purchaser

From 'Treasure Island'

If sailor tales to sailor tunes,
  Storm and adventure, heat and cold,
If schooners, islands, and maroons
  And Buccaneers and buried Gold,
And all the old romance, retold
  Exactly in the ancient way,
Can please, as me they pleased of old,
  The wiser youngsters of today:
So be it, and fall on! If not,
  If studious youth no longer crave,
His ancient appetites forgot,
  Kingston, or Ballantyne the brave,
Or Cooper of the wood and wave:
  So be it, also! And may I
And all my pirates share the grave
  Where these and their creations lie!

Pirate Ditty

from 'Treasure Island'

Fifteen men on the Dead Man's Chest –
   Yo-ho-ho, and a bottle of rum!
Drink and the devil had done for the rest –
   Yo-ho-ho, and a bottle of rum!

The Song of the Sword of Alan
from 'Kidnapped'

This is the song of the sword of Alan:
The smith made it,
The fire set it;
Now it shines in the hand of Alan Breck.

Their eyes were many and bright,
Swift were they to behold,
Many the hand they guided:
The sword was alone.

The dun deer troop over the hill,
They are many, the hill is one:
The dun deer vanish,
The hill remains.

Come to me from the hills of heather,
Come from the isles of the sea.
O far-beholding eagles,
Here is your meat.

To Katharine de Mattos

With a copy of 'Dr Jekyll and Mr Hyde'

Bells upon the city are ringing in the night;
High above the gardens are the houses full of light;
On the heathy Pentlands is the curfew flying free,
And the broom is blowing bonnie in the north
  countrie.

It's ill to break the bonds that God decreed to bind,
Still we'll be the children of the heather and the wind.
Far away from home, O, it's still for you and me
That the broom is blowing bonnie in the north
  countrie!

To My Wife

Found in the Manuscript of 'Weir of Hermiston'

I saw rain falling and the rainbow drawn
On Lammermuir. Hearkening I heard again
In my precipitous city beaten bells
Winnow the keen sea wind. And here afar,
Intent on my own race and place, I wrote.

    Take thou the writing: thine it is. For who
Burnished the sword, blew on the drowsy coal,
Held still the target higher, chary of praise
And prodigal of censure – who but thou?
So now, in the end, if this the least be good,
If any deed be done, if any fire
Burn in the imperfect page, the praise be thine.

On an Inland Voyage

Who would think, herein to look,
That from these exiguous bounds,
I have dug a printed book
And a cheque for twenty pounds?

Thus do those who trust the Lord
Go rejoicing on their way
And receive a great reward
For having been so kind as lay.

Had the fun of the voyage
Had the sport of the boats
Who could have hoped in addition
The pleasure of fing'ring the notes?

Yes, sir, I wrote the book; I own the fact
It was, perhaps, sir, an unworthy act.
Have you perused it, sir? – You have? – indeed
Then between you and me there no debate is.
I did a silly act, but I was fee'd;
You did a sillier, and you did it gratis!

On Some Ghostly
Companions at A Spa

That was an evil day when I
To Strathpeffer drew anigh,
For there I found no human soul
But Ogres occupied the whole.

They had at first a human air
In coats and flannel underwear.
They rose and walked upon their feet
And filled their bellies full of meat.
They wiped their lips when they had done,
But they were Ogres every one.

Each issuing from his secret bower,
I marked them in the morning hour.
By limp and totter, lisp and droop,
I singled each one from the group.
I knew them all as they went by –
I knew them by their blasted eye!

Detested Ogres, from my sight
Depart to your congenial night!
From these fair vales, from this fair day,
Fleet, spectres, on your downward way,
Like changing figures in a dream,
To Muttonhold or Pittenweem!
As, by some harmony divine
The devils quartered in the swine,
If any baser place exist

In God's great registration list –
Some den with wallow and a trough –
Find it, ye ogres, and be off!

from Brasheanna

Sonnets on Peter Brash, a publican, dedicated to Charles Baxter

3

There let us often wend our pensive way,
  There often pausing celebrate the past;
  For though indeed our BRASH be dead at last,
Perchance his spirit, in some minor way,
Nor pure immortal nor entirely dead,
  Contrives upon the farther shore of death
  To pick a rank subsistence, and for breath
Breathes ague, and drinks creosote of lead,
There, on the way to that infernal den,
  Where burst the flames forth thickly, and the sky
    Flares horrid through the murk methinks he doles
    Damned liquors out to Hellward-faring souls,
  And as his impotent anger ranges high
Gibbers and gurgles at the shades of men.

Chronology of Stevenson's Life

Year	Age	Life
1850		Born 13 November in Edinburgh, only child of Margaret Isabella Balfour and Thomas Stevenson, lighthouse and harbour engineer
1857	7	The family moves to 17 Heriot Row. Stevenson's schooling sporadic as he is often ill
1867	17	To Edinburgh University to study engineering, later law, though hopes to become a writer
1873	23	Meets Sidney Colvin friend and mentor, and first serious love, Fanny Sitwell. First article published
1875	25	Meets W. E. Henley, friend and collaborator. Called to the Scottish bar. First visit to Fontainebleau, France
1876	26	Meets Fanny Osbourne
1878	28	First book, *An Inland Voyage*, published
1879	29	Follows Fanny to California. *Travels with a Donkey* published. Growing recognition as a writer

Chronology of his Times

Year	Age	Life
1880	30	Marries Fanny, returns to Scotland. Until 1884 spends winters in Switzerland and France for his health, summers in Scotland
1881	31	*Virginibus Puerisque* (essays) published
1882	32	*Familiar Studies of Men and Books* (essays) and *New Arabian Nights* published
1883	33	*Treasure Island* and *The Silverado Squatters* published. Recognition as fiction writer
1884	34	Moves to Bournemouth. Forms close friendship with Henry James
1885	35	*A Child's Garden of Verses* and *Prince Otto* published
1886	36	*Strange Case of Dr Jekyll and Mr Hyde* published; bestseller. *Kidnapped* published to critical acclaim
1887	37	Death of Thomas Stevenson. To USA; winter in Adirondack Mountains. *Underwoods* and *Memories and Portraits* (essays) published
1888	38	First South Pacific voyage. Health in yacht *Casco* much improved. Draws on Pacific experiences for articles and fiction. *The Master of Ballantrae* and *The Black Arrow* published
1889	39	Six months in Hawaii; voyage on schooner *Equator*. *The Wrong Box*, written with stepson Lloyd Osbourne, published
1890	40	Voyage on *Janet Nichol*. Settles at Vailima, island of Upolu, Samoa. *Ballads* published

Year	Literary Context	Historical Events
1880		William Ewart Gladstone becomes prime minister
1881	Death of Thomas Carlyle	Death of Disraeli First Boer War breaks out Alexander III becomes Tsar of Russia
1882	Publication begins of *Dictionary of National Biography*	Pretoria Convention ends Boer War Triple Alliance formed between Italy, Austria and Germany
1884	Publication begins of the *Oxford English Dictionary*	Fabian Society founded Third Reform Act passed
1885		Earl of Salisbury becomes prime minister
1886	Hardy, *The Mayor of Casterbridge*	First Irish Home Rule Bill fails
1887		Queen Victoria's Golden Jubilee
1888	August Strindberg produces *Miss Julie*	Jack the Ripper murders six women in London William II becomes German emperor
1889	W. B. Yeats, *The Wanderings of Oisin*	
1890		Bismarck is dismissed as chancellor Henri de Toulouse-Lautrec produces first Moulin Rouge paintings

Year	Age	Life
1890–94		At Vailima with Fanny and extended family. Writes work inspired by both the Pacific and Scotland. *In the South Seas* published
1892	42	*The Wrecker* (with Lloyd Osbourne) and *A Footnote to History* published
1893	43	*Catriona* published
1894	44	Dies 3 December of cerebral haemorrhage leaving *Weir of Hermiston* and *St Ives* unfinished

Year	Literary Context	Historical Events
1891		Paul Gauguin settles in Tahiti
1892	Oscar Wilde produces *Lady Windermere's Fan*	
1893		Second Irish Home Rule Bill fails
		Civil war breaks out in Samoa
1894	Kipling, *The Jungle Book* du Maurier, *Trilby*	Earl of Rosebery becomes prime minister

DATE DUE

GAYLORD   PRINTED IN U.S.A.